Theme Restaurant Design

Entertainment & Fun Dining

Martin M. Pagler

Retail Reporting Corporation, New York

Retail Reporting Corporation
302 Fifth Avenue
New York, NY 10001

Distributors to the trade in the United States and Canada
McGraw-Hill, Inc.
1221 Avenue of the Americas
New York, NY 10020

Distributors outside the United States and Canada
Hearst Books International
1350 Avenue of the Americas
New York, NY 10019

Library of Congress Cataloging in Publication Data:
Theme Restaurant Design

Printed in Hong Kong
ISBN 0-934590-87-7

Book Design: Harish Patel Design Associates

Table of Contents

Introduction

Martin M. Pegler

Centuries ago Shakespeare wrote that "All the world is a stage," and more recently Dietz & Schwartz, the songwriters, put it to music when they penned, "The world is a stage—and the stage is the world of Entertainment." If you pick up any trade publication concerning the retail, mall development or restaurant/hospitality fields, you are sure to find an article on "The Entertainment Factor"—and how it relates to success in today's business ventures.

In the 1980s and '90s we have become a nation of pleasure seekers; of people in need of constant stimulation—instant gratification—searching for the flickering lights, the action, the excitement—the sparkle, glitter, glamour and glitz in the world. We are on an unending roller coaster ride demanding "highs." We want to live in a world as envisioned and executed by Disney; everything picture-perfect and everything colorful, bright and "sunny side up."

We fondly remember "the good old days": the days before we were born but that we see as virtual reality through a golden gauze, all lovely, lush and illuminated with rosy light of remembrance. When we shop we want to have "fun." When we dine we want to be amused, entertained, bombarded with images, sights and smells. We want to be transported in time—in space—and to any and all parts of the world—and we want to be fed exotic foods in exotic surroundings.

The "abra cadabra" word is THEME. Theme or Thematic Design is one way retail and restaurant designers are providing the desired entertainment for today's consumers. A theme is "a melody that is repeated or on which variations are constructed." Theme is a subject: a time—a place—a state of mind and with variations it can become an environment rich in details, memorabilia—and an escape from reality. The theme is the launching pad into a flight of fancy and fantasy. The theme concept—as a source of entertainment and wonderment is not new. It existed well before Disneyland and Disneyworld, but Disney did give the concept new meaning—a new depth of expression, and showed how one could turn reality into fantasy; the humdrum into humor; and how to color the world with light and a palette of rainbow colors.

This book is a collection of some of the most noted theme restaurants in the U.S.—and the world. Whether the theme is Hollywood and the Movies, the golden age of Rock 'n' Roll or Motown, Radio and TV; Sports and Sporting Events; Ecology and the World Around Us; Travel and Transportation—we have gathered examples such as Hard Rock Cafe, Planet Hollywood, Motown, Rainforest Cafe, Dive!, Michael Jordan's, The All-Star Cafe—and many, many more. In addition there are the themed restaurants where the accent is on foreign foods and foreign lands. Often the stage is the Exhibition Kitchen—open to viewing from any seat in the restaurant. A cast of cuisine artistes perform their culinary theatrics whisking, blending, stirring, shaking, flambé-ing, flipping, stripping, carving, or just cavorting with roasted carcasses—all the while catering to our curious eyes and whetting our appetites. From buffets and sushi bars to stir-fry and simmer at your table, to sit-down service, we have included notable examples of the restaurant designers' art and their ability to capture and keep the diners' interest while solving the requirements of an efficient working food service.

Theme restaurants come in all sizes and are designed for all ages; from the teens and twenties who revel in Planet Hollywood and the Hard Rock Cafe—to their yuppie parents who still remember Dick Clark's American Bandstand—to those even older who grew up on the turkey, giblet gravy and lumpy mashed potatoes served in the silvery diners of the '50s. There is a theme—and a dream for everyone. Whether your memories are of horror films on Saturday matinees—or the glamour of Tinseltown in the '40s—or if you want the laid-back down-country Bayou background of a Tib's Fleamarket—or you want to travel in style at Clydes—or just thrill to the underwater adventure at Dive!—we've added them to this collection for your perusal, your pleasure and your entertainment. "That's Entertainment."

Theme Restaurant Design

Entertainment & Fun Dining

- *Hollywood & the Movies*

- *Music: Records, Radio and TV*

- *Sports and Sporting Events*

- *Travel: Trains, Planes and Steamers*

- *Time: The Good Old Days*

- *Ecology and the World Around Us*

Dive!
Las Vegas, NV

Design: *Meisel Associates, Ltd., Chicago, IL*
Idletime, Orlando, FL

A life-size yellow and purple nose of a submarine rises up and comes "crashing" through a 30 ft. wall of water in the desert of Las Vegas! It is not an invasion—it is just the next generation of Dive!—a dining/entertainment concept—moving into the glitter gulch of the Las Vegas scene. With the success of the Los Angeles Dive! (reviewed in Cafes & Coffee Houses) comes this next one in the planned flotilla of subs heading across the country. The exterior sub nose explodes through the water wall which cascades into an oversized pool which randomly blasts off "synchronized depth charges." The nose includes six ballast blow holes that emit water and there are 12 fog misters at the "scupper" drains. It is topped with an up periscope and radar light. Fiber optic accents surround the entire "sub" and outline the four color Dive! logo on the conning tower.

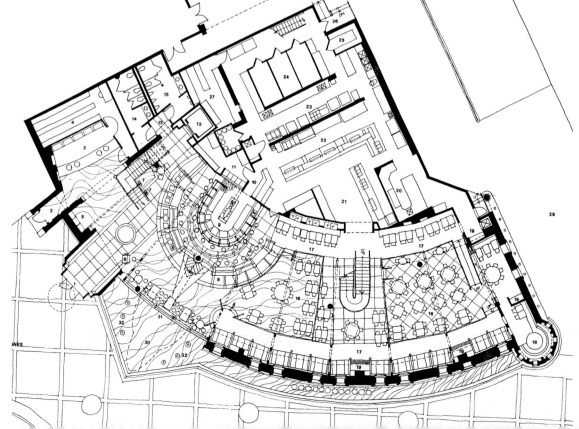

Dive!

A 35-ft. lighthouse, at the far end, welcomes guests with its working beacon. Between the nose and the lighthouse, the body of the restaurant is painted gunmetal gray and accented with nine porthole shaped bubble windows and neon trim.

A team of architects, designers and consultants blended real and imaginary sub decor with special effects to create the interior of Dive! Meisel Associates, Ltd. of Chicago and Idletime of Orlando, FL worked together to coordinate the interior design with the special effects.

The body of the 16,000 sq. ft., two story restaurant replicates the hull of a sub with vaulted cylindrical ceilings and bowed exterior walls braced by ribs. A variety of metal materials were used, painted in accent colors, and overhead is a network of technical, sub operation details include exposed conduits, pressure gauges, throttles, control panels, sonar screens and a bathysphere suspended from the ceiling.

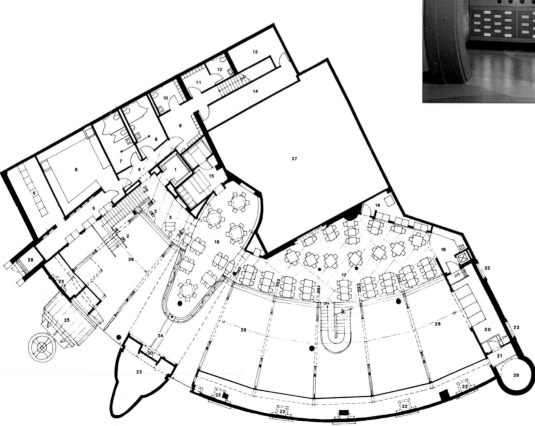

Principle in Charge:
Joe Meisel

Photography:
Doug Snower

Every 30 minutes a computerized Dive! show simulates the experience of an actual dive and the video screens turn into a wash of water as the sub submerges. Seating on the first level borders the galley—the kitchen—while the above "sea-level" provides an overall view of the submarine. All dining booths are separated by glass-back panels etched with a "traveling" Dive! sub. "Periscopes" located on the "sub" can be viewed to look out onto the Strip—or to "spy" on other diners. A 16 cube video wall, in the rear of the sub, "creates a seamless projection surface." The rear projection screen, visible from both levels, features a Dive! underwater adventure as do the additional monitors spaced throughout the interior.

Larry Levy, chairperson of Levy Restaurants and one of the partners of Dive! said, "The atmosphere we've created allows guests to escape to a completely uncharted environment—one that combines the tastes of wonderful submarine sandwiches with breakthrough decor and special effects which celebrate the food concept."

Motown Cafe
W. 57th St., New York, NY

Design:
Haverson Architecture & Design
Greenwich, CT

Joining the long line of entertainment/eateries on W. 57th St.—and those just off that street—is the Motown cafe that opened in what was a noted art deco Horn & Hardart Automat. The design team conceived a distinct design identity for this flagship location based on the "excitement, the dynamism and the driving artistic energy of the Motown sound."

A 20-ft. beacon, resembling a radio tower, rises off the roof of the 1930s structure and five foot tall, internally illuminated letters and five radiant stars spell out Motown atop the parapet. The original glazed terra cotta facade was restored and a new stainless steel canopy and revolving door were added.

Some of the interior spaces were gutted, but some were maintained and enhanced such as the paneled ceiling, stepping pilaster columns, and the "wonderfully expressive" glazed terra cotta stairway that connects the street level with the mezzanine.

In keeping with the various component elements of the Motown sound, the Cafe is divided into distinct areas of visual interest: "reflecting the different elements of music,

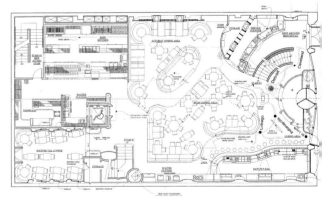

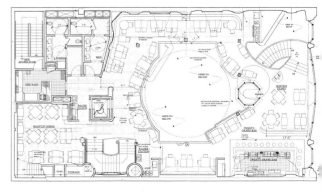

lyrics, production and artistry." A series of "vignettes" make up a "contrasting, yet integrated, visual whole and are stylistically representative of actual places in the lives of artists in their rise to fame." The warm and friendly, yet dynamic, ambience is created with design roots in the architecture of the 1950s and '60s.

Up front, a circular platform with yellow Motown letters and stars embedded in a blue terrazzo field shows off a collection of Motown "icons" on several different levels: the Supremes in the foreground, the marquee and stage

announcing "Motown Revue Live Tonight," and a nearly 30-ft. spinning record over the stage. "The key elements to the success of Motown sound were style, movement and sound."

A "map" at the visitors feet highlights the locations such as Chicago, St. Louis, Indianapolis and Cleveland, and directs patrons to the Motown Bar, the main dining room, the Automat, Roostertail Lounge, Stairway to Success, Twenty Grand Bar/Lounge, Mezzanine Lounge, Rooftop Dining, and the souvenir shop—Shop Around.

The Motown Bar is curvilinear and streamlined and constructed of '60s materials like aluminum, stainless steel, glass block and blonde woods. Artifacts, photos, sheets of music and candid shots soften the effect.

The main dining room area, in platinum, gold, ruby red, teal, Motown blue and chamois, is the design focus of the Cafe. A 45 rpm disk over 35 ft. in diameter— with the Motown label—spins over the dining area. The lighting is warm: a combination of indirect cove illumination plus pin spots that highlight the memorabilia and record covers that line the perimeter walls.

Based on one of Detroit's "hottest clubs" is Roostertail Lounge in black, gold, and dark burled maple. This area, which can be closed off for private parties, is decked out with formal portraits of the great Motown artists. The Twenty Grand Bar/Lounge was conceived as a piece of living American musical history, and it recreates the legendary Detroit lounge that featured many rising Motown stars.

The red quilted curvilinear bar is capped with mahogany and period green velour, sofa-like banquettes "centers" this part of the mezzanine plan. The Mezzanine Lounge has banqueted areas for dining and a multi-media gallery of video projections. The metallic cranberry red and patinaed silver leafed walls are a background for the Motown artists rehearsing or appearing at the Apollo Theater in New York City's Harlem.

Blonde woods, black trim and terrazzo floors create a contrast for the merchandise for sale in Shop Around—a two story retail shop on the main and lower level. Customers can enter from the main waiting room near the entrance or directly through a double door on the street.

Architect:
Jay Haverson

Graphic Designer:
Carolyn Haverson

Design Team:
Ingunn Haraldson, David Jablonka, Ken Anderson, Sven Levine, Chris Ruehl, Michael Gonzaga, Deborah Olchowski, Lisa Bianco, Michael Kaufman, Palmer Ramstad

Design Consultants:
Richard Baskin & John Jerde, Los Angeles, CA

Photography:
Paul Warchol, Warchol Photography

Facade:
Matthew Lawn

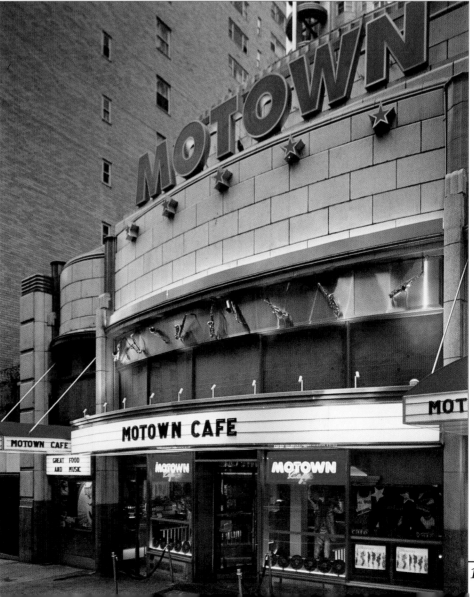

It's a "really b-i-i-i-g show" at the Sullivan's Restaurant located in the Ed Sullivan Theater on Broadway in New York City. Once the home of "legitimate theater" and then for many years the place for Ed Sullivan's popular variety TV shows, it now shares its space with David Letterman's late time TV shows. This restaurant celebrates theater—and TV broadcasting.

What was once an Irish bar is now a 25 ft. high interior—all curves and pure drama. The TV/fishbowl that serves as the maitre d's station is "the first cue to visual theater" in the restaurant.

The imposing dark mahogany bar on the "orchestra" or main level is located under a large mirror and between the parted curtains. In feeling, it recalls the Irish bar "heritage." The balance of this level combines terrazzo floors, beveled and etched mirrors with booth seating tucked under the stairs. The grand staircase leads to the loge where the balcony space is terraced with a variety of tables and banquettes. This upper level culminates in the final row of "power" booths. These classic half round banquettes are called "Hollywoods."

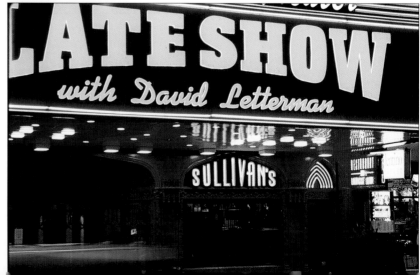

A reproduction of the original red velvet curtain from the Ed Sullivan Theater recreates the feel and scale of the proscenium as it reaches 25 ft. in height and 50 ft. across. The red curtains are echoed at the rear of the balcony by the custom print wallpaper drapes for each power booth. The designers' attitude towards the technical and service functions was to "replicate" what might have existed in the 1930s and '40s. Sprinkler pipes are exposed and painted, but the HVAC, wherever possible is hidden behind grilles. Lighting imitates "stage lighting" techniques and technology.

The actual performance stage is situated above the glassed-in entrance foyer on the interior "marquee." The sound system is visually related to the live performances and the acoustics are more subdued upstairs, especially near the power booths where carpet has been laid.

"Sullivan's captures the spirit and essence of entertainment in a restaurant that is 'a theater within a theatre.'"

Project Architect:
James Biber, AIA

Asst. Architects:
Michael Zweck Bronner
& James Cleary

Photography:
Peter Mauss/Esto

Dick Clark's American Bandstand Grill
Columbus, OH

Design:
Design Development Interior
Design, Tarzana, CA

Almost as American as "apple pie" is the perennial Dick Clark, and his name is synonymous with American Bandstand which for over three decades has been a mainstay for teenagers watching TV. This is where they learned to dance—to dress—and to appreciate the artists of rock 'n' roll. The program was both an important reflection of, and contributor to, American pop culture through the "baby boomers'" formative years. The American Bandstand Grill celebrates the legacy of the TV show, and the menu—"The Great American Food Experience"— includes regional recipes from all across the U.S. Memorabilia from American Bandstand and pop music history are part of the dining experience in the Grill where stage costumes, original work contracts, gold records and signed memorabilia line the walls and add a nostalgic touch and a reflection of the "loss of innocence" and a time that once was.

Central to the design is the circle: the record disk and the original Bandstand dance floor that is recreated here under a neon illuminated circular cove with theatrical lighting "lost" in the darkness.

The interior is warm, woody and nostalgic. The area in front of the bar has a black and white mosaic ceramic tile "keyboard" laid into the wooden floor.

In the "diner-like" seating area where ochers, persimmons and beiges are mixed with light and dark wood, the carpet is patterned with a design of "records," some bearing the American Bandstand (AB) logo. The same logo, neon illuminated, is part of the "stacked record" facade/entrance design and it also appears over the bar. In the apse ending, around the circular dance floor where guests can dance to music that spans the last five decades, there is more booth seating up against the curved wall of windows.

Inside the Grill, patrons are invited to take a walk down the "Walk of Fame": a foyer lined with glass cases containing mementoes of the rock 'n' roll great. Throughout the dining experience, the visitor is literally surrounded by memorabilia from Dick Clark's own personal collection. Diners are also entertained by the state-of-the-art technology that not only provides the dance music but through a network of monitors spaced around the Grill allows them to see hundred of Bandstand clips or hear over 4000 song titles through the studio-quality sound system.

The All American Menu combines "express" items with more leisurely dining options and a good selection of "lighter" offerings. In addition, guests can take home a piece of American Bandstand with souvenirs that range from sweatshirts, tee shirts, caps and jackets to coffee mugs, key rings and cassettes.

Design Team:
Eddy Bitton,
Ron Lieberman,
David Lieberman

Photography:
Michael Houghton

Established as a "fun-filled, kick-up-your-heels, family environment" with an all-American fare, Country Star is a restaurant/country music entertainment center situated in entertainment filled Universal City. The 15,000 sq. ft. dining experience space is loaded with memorabilia, videos, and in-house live performances. The giant juke box facade—all neon and radiant —acts as "an embracing beacon to patrons" and the projecting marquee gives shelter to those patiently waiting to get in.

The interior look is quickly established by the rustic rock formations and the domed rotunda that is illuminated like a star-filled, desert sky. A giant wall of video monitors and display niches is complemented by the terrazzo star "Walk of Fame" that leads visitors to the dining rooms that follow.

Because of the sloping terrain of the plot, the architect/design firm—Hatch Design Group— divided the vast dining room into curvilinear, individual dining zones with banquettes and free-standing tables that accommodate up to 50 patrons in each. They are a "playful blending of styles seeking to create numerous settings within one space." In one

Design:
Jeff Hatch, Bill Cole, Kimberly Gee, Jackie Hanson, Todd Hatch, Donna Kruse, Ben Pollock, Diane Varney

Photography: Cameron Carothers

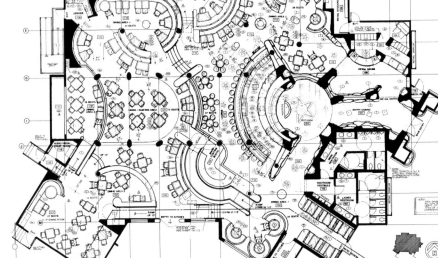

EQUIPMENT FLOOR PLAN : DINING AREA

zone, a classic diner sets the theme for the exposition kitchen facade and the tables surrounding it.

Walls, glazed in Grand Canyon hues, become the background for the myriad country memorabilia, and the terrazzo floors, in "saturated sunset" colors, flow freely throughout only to be interrupted by the large wood dance floor. The booths are upholstered in embellished leather and vinyl, trimmed with nailheads and concho accents.

The artifacts are presented in stylish displayers made of rich woods highlighted with leather and chrome. Even the column enclosures become animated with fanciful cowboy boots of polished or brushed stainless steel. At the center of the main room, behind the stage, is a mural depicting the source of Country music. A retail shop provides the souvenirs that patrons want to remember their visit.

Michael Jordan's Chicago, IL

Design:
Zakaspace
Ft. Lauderdale, FL

Michael Jordan's is more than a restaurant-it is an entertainment complex and the newest dining/entertainment mecca for visitors to Chicago. The old brick building on No. LaSalle is topped with an 18 ft. diameter basketball and the three levels, inside, divide the building into the bar, the dining room and the banquet facilities by floors.

From under the black canopied central entrance, the visitor has a view of the bar and the retail shop as well as the stairwell that reveals the second and third floors. The impressive bar combines an industrial feeling with some high tech elements. Cast iron column and beams are painted chrome yellow and accented by a row of cobalt blue runway lights. The 20x6 ft., state-of-the-art, multiple screen monitor that fills most of the wall behind the bar shows customized video programs as well as sporting events. The red and black vinyl seats are arranged on three tiers as to simulate stadium seating and this also allows for viewing throughout the space. Black brick shaped tiles are used on the floor and from the ceiling are suspended contemporary black fans and industrial-style

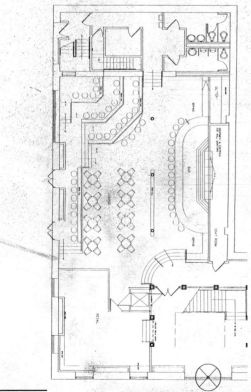

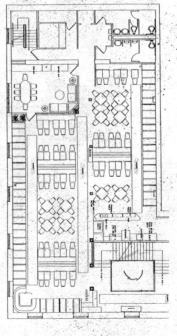

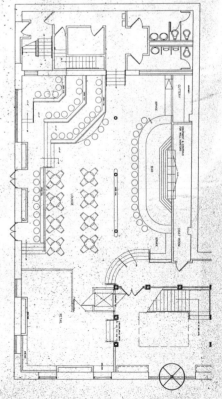

pendant, red lighting fixtures. A wall is dedicated to magazine covers featuring Michael Jordan and other memorabilia, in illuminated museum-style cases, that line the wall.

The main dining room, on the second level, can be accessed by the main staircase or by elevator. The focal element here is the food buffet, refrigerated ingredients, and the espresso/cappuccino makers in the center of the room. The walls are paneled up to six feet with a light colored mahogany and the cove lighting above it throws a golden light onto the very contemporary artwork of Greg Cove just under the ceiling. Framed Michael Jordan magazine covers also decorate the wood walls.

The original black and white ceramic mosaic tiled floor has been preserved and the space is warmed by the long oriental runners in the walkways and the chocolate brown naugehyde covered banquettes and chairs. Overscaled white globes hang from the ceiling and with the high tech track lighting illuminate the room. The white table cloths also reflect the light. There is a lounge/living room area on this level with a large built-in wall unit with shelves lined with many of Jordan's trophies, awards and other memorabilia.

The top level is a banquet space that can be divided into smaller private areas. A high, wide open wood truss ceiling overhead is filled with over-scaled half-globe chandeliers. The artwork, mostly of the basketball playing Bulls and other Chicago sports teams, is colorful and festive and reaffirms the sports focus of Michael Jordan's.

Photography:
Mark Ballogg,
Steinkamp/Ballogg

Design:
Engstrom Design Group
San Raphael, CA

Working with the Harrah's Entertainment Group, the Engstrom Design Group came up with Winning Streaks, a national sports restaurant/bar concept. With the North Kansas City property, the designers had the opportunity to start from the ground up. They created a free-standing, 2900 sq. ft. restaurant modeled after the 1914 Ebbet's Field ballpark in Brooklyn: a mini-stadium with old world brickwork, arched multipane windows and steel bleacher supports.

Inside, visual cues build on the old stadium atmosphere. Second story "grandstands" are "peopled" with two dimensional painted wood "fans." Replica field lights are set against the "sky" ceiling that changes from daytime to night-time. There are railings patterned after the galvanized barriers in Brigg's Stadium in Detroit, and sports events are featured from a custom designed "scoreboard" with eight TV monitors and programmable neon sculpture.

Custom carpeting, in the main dining room, reflects the color and markings of a football field while some dining tables are set out on a "basketball court" wooden floor—complete with hoop. High bar tables, on a decorative mosaic tile floor, are positioned on the opposite side of the circular space. Cutting through the center of the room is a "shuffleboard court" that serves as a dance floor. A video "control booth" doubles as a disc jockey station when the sports programs are concluded for the night.

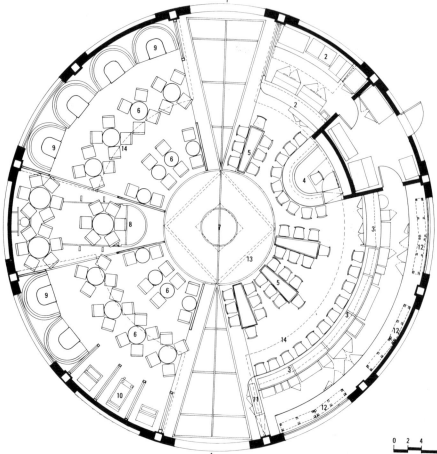

0 2 4
feet

Part of the entertainment and environment is the exhibition kitchen. The gray walls are accented with red, blue, yellow and white, and industrial-type pendants (some with grill covers) add light and ambience. Authentic Streak memorabilia, custom banners with quotes from famous record holders, sports TV programming and interactive sports games add to the color, the dazzle and the excitement of Winning Streak—and invite guests "to participate in the many emotions of winning."

Design Team:
Eric Engstrom, Jennifer Johanson, Kathy Hallal

Architect:
Hnedak Bobo Group, Memphis, TN

Photography:
Hank Young

Official All Star Cafe
Times Square, New York, NY

Design:
Rockwell Group
New York, NY

Adding to the glitter, glitz and overall excitement of Times Square in New York City, is the newly-opened Official All Star Cafe on a 40,000 sq. ft. location on Broadway and W. 45th St. This cafe is part of the Urban Entertainment Destination project which includes a 65,000 sq. ft. Virgin Megastore and a four-plex Sony theater next door. The celebration of sports and sporting events starts on the outside as lines of eager fans snake around the corner waiting to get in.

Designed by the Rockwell Group, noted for many fabled entertainment/eateries such as Planet Hollywood, "The Official All Star Cafe is a rich, fun-filled sports environment that provides patrons with a visceral sense of being there." The 20,000 sq. ft. interior space is arena shaped—like a stadium—and can accommodate up to 800 patrons between the restaurant and bar areas.

The main floor is covered with grass-like carpeting—to recall outdoor stadiums—while other floors are finished in rubber tiles, or wood that suggest sports playing areas such as the half basketball court marked off on the wood floor of the bar. "Our design for this project takes the use of technology as entertainment to a new strata in its state-of-the-art application to interactive TV and virtual reality video."

Specially-orchestrated video segments "book-end and link" the live sports feeds from the networks, cable channels, international satellite with celebrity interviews right within the restaurant. While actual games in progress are not displayed in the main dining area, they can be viewed in private dining facilities. An on-site V.J. (video jockey) is equipped with myriad sports clips with which to provide "non obtrusive video wallpaper" overhead in the simulated stadium 360 degree surround of video screens.

Enhancing the "sporting event" experience are the glove leather seats, the simulated raceway bar and the prominently-displayed sports memorabilia in the re-invented stadium. Among the stellar attractions are Shaq O'Neal's broken backboard, some famous racing cars and items provided by sports stars such as Andre Agassi, Wayne Gretzky, Ken Griffey Jr., and Joe Montana.

In addition, there is a retail shop for sports-related souvenirs and clothing.

Photography:
Norman McGrath

Way up near the roof of the GM Place Sporting Arena was a dark, long, narrow space of 6600 sq. ft. that had been set aside to serve as a restaurant/lounge facility. The windows in the perimeter walls were not features to the space nor were the views of the outdoors worth capitalizing on.

Working within a limited budget, Sunderland Innerspace Design designed a warm and comfortable environment that is open to the entire length to the arena bowl for viewing. A large peninsular bar was positioned perpendicular to the space to break up the length of the room. This created a sense of intimacy and also generated excitement as the secondary focal point in the the lounge. When there is nothing going on in the arena below, the bar is where the action is.

Close to the bar is an internally-illuminated rear autograph wall-conceived for signatures and comments of visiting sports figures and celebrities. Trophy cases are integrated into this millwork and glass showcase framing. Photographic memorabilia of the home sports teams further the sports theme of the grille.

Important to the design of the room is the mural in the raised ceiling depicting the various sporting events that take place in the arena. The ceiling change occurs with a gentle slope and the mural bleeds in to the main, lightly-colored, gypsum board wall surface. The colors are picked up from the finishes used in the space.

Accentuating the lower level viewing gallery and the grille's location are seven foot tall wood-carved, active sports figures. The table arrangements for both viewing galleries are developed around five foot half-round tables cantilevered with steel supports reinforced from the stub walls. The west end of the restaurant features a glass enclosed exhibition kitchen with a long cooking line. "It adds activity and entertainment to the decor."

Planet Hollywood
San Diego, CA & Orlando, FL

Design:
Rockwell Group
New York, NY

A phenomenon of the '90s— like the Hard Rock Cafe was of the '80s—is Planet Hollywood; part restaurant, part cafe, part museum and part retail outlet. It is the "in" place for persons of all ages who love the movies, nostalgia, being where "the action" is and being a part of "the action." Every new Planet Hollywood opening has all the drama, pizzazz and glamour of the old time movie premiere where a succession of film and entertainment notables show up to show off.

"The central idea for Planet Hollywood designs," says David Rockwell of Rockwell Group who designs these multi-media extravaganzas, "is that of creating a world in which Hollywood icons are brought to life and the patrons feel as though they're stepping right into the movies with them." This approach has resulted in a series of strongly themed casual restaurants brimming over with Hollywood memorabilia in places such as New York, Aspen, Washington, DC, Las Vegas, London and Chicago.

By incorporating such one-of-a-kind collections of artifacts in every available space of the informal, relaxed restaurants, each location's collection is "a unique architectural event" to be participated in by the observer.

Depending upon the location, themed rooms are developed that speak to the particular locale. In London, the diner enters through a "gun barrel" into the James Bond room while the "Gangster Speakeasy Parlor" in Chicago has walls riddled with bullet holes. A science fiction room is carried over from location to location "as a testimony to the role of fantasy and adventure in movie lore." In almost all Planet Hollywoods the central focus is the main dining room and the "diorama of the Hollywood Hills with its singular combination of imagery, nostalgia, memorabilia and lighting effects."

Planet Hollywood's menu features prepared dishes which have become the backbone of California's new classic cuisine—unusual pastas, exotic salads, turkey burgers, gourmet pizzas, a selection of smoked and grilled meats and fish, a variety of vegetarian offerings, as well as a range of desserts.

A full line of Planet Hollywood clothing is available in every Planet Hollywood merchandise shop. Items including hats, tee shirts, sweatshirts, watches, boxer shorts, denim and leather jackets, and other specialty items are on sale to guests that want to take a piece of Planet Hollywood home with them.

Photography:
Norman McGrath

Something BIG—really BIG—and exciting and dazzling and super theatrical has opened in Grand Rapids that is unlike anything that has ever appeared there before. The Amway Grand Plaza Hotel now features a new, two-level, 244-seat, Tinseltown restaurant. Combining Hollywood and Music themes, the space is a salute to Hollywood and the entire entertainment industry. According to Joe Tomaselli, president of Amway Hotel Corp., Tinseltown has "great food and a fun and entertaining atmosphere to create a unique experience for guests."

The host's stand—upon entering—was inspired by the 1950s movie ticket booth, and also up front—where patrons can browse—is a retail area with Tinseltown branded merchandise. There is a Menu Revue available that is a tabloid size newspaper that in addition to telling of the food offerings, includes juicy tidbits of Hollywood trivia. With a five screen video tower hovering over it, the circular bar can accommodate 26 patrons. A giant star intersected by a guitar—the restaurant's logo—stretches across most of the length of the lower level's ceiling. An 11 by 14 video wall of six screens is another focal point which also entertains guests at this level seated either at the bar or at the table and booths.

More secluded dining is available on the upper level where a blue domed ceiling with 1200 fiber optic "stars" gives the feeling of dining under a night sky. Here, the open kitchen provides the entertainment and the setting includes several wood burning ovens and a large stainless steel marquee over the kitchen opening. Video monitors, at ceiling height around the room's perimeter, offer another form of entertainment—or distraction.

Film and music memorabilia including classic record album covers and movie stills decorate the walls of Tinseltown along with the spectacular neon artwork created by Neon Design of Chicago. With the changing music format, the 360 CD "Jukebox," the video monitors showing clips from old movies as well as current sporting events and news broadcasts over satellite, Tinseltown—as designed by Aumiller Youngquist of Mt. Pleasant—captures the essence of Hollywood in its heyday.

Principal:
David Kasprak

Project Architects:
Marc Nix

Project Design Team:
Karen Reinger, Roy Huang

Photography:
Mark Ballogg, Steinkamp/Ballogg, Chicago, IL

There has always been a fascination with the unknown, the "macabre, with death" and so movies and TV shows have dwelt on the dealt with "Horror." "Horror" is now the theme for the fun, Jekyll & Hyde, entertainment/eatery which joins many other theme-filled restaurants.

berg Kolb of New York, the space unfolds on four levels with a dramatic five-story atrium assuring diners, on all levels, that they can participate in the "skullduggery" and "dastardly deeds" going on in this "English Gentlemen's Club." Each floor has a specific theme—the Grand Salon—the Library—and the wood and leathery "antique" interior is taxed with "trophies" from expeditions to mysterious places or the hunt. Sphinxes, animal heads and Polynesian masks not only bedeck the walls, they move, talk and tell jokes while interacting with the diners.

Throughout, the designers have used real materials to create the desired ambience; mahogany, limestone, wrought iron fences used as balcony rails, spiralling metal staircases exposed rather than hidden in unseen tunnels, patterned carpets, elaborate fabrics and ornate moldings. Skeletons, dressed in period clothes, frequent the Victorian bar and also appear, unexpectedly, in other places. Adding to the theatrical feeling are the stage lights that seem to be everywhere.

Actors roam the floors dressed as chambermaids, aviators and mad scientists and they involve the guests in their strange, staged scenes. The dining experience culminates in an elaborate light, sound and floor show starring Dr. Jekyll, Mr. Hyde and a guest appearance by Frankenstein. The towering atrium allows sightlines throughout and also serves as the stage at ground level.

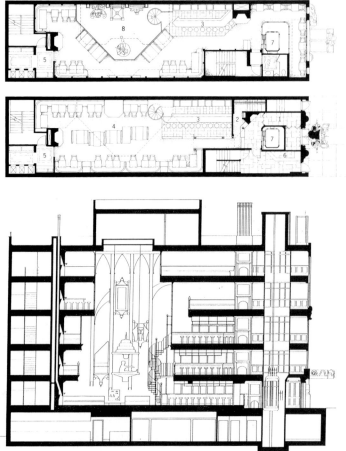

Design:
Eric Rosenberg &
Michele Kolb

Special Effects &
Lighting:
Dan Hoffman

Facade Construction:
MJM Studios

Photography:
Nathan Sayers

Now it can be Halloween every night of the year and the "locals" can enjoy being spooked and shivered anytime of the year.

Based on the TV "cult" show—The Night Gallery—a voyage into the eerie, the spooky and the weird—the paintings that opened each weekly segment are now used to provide the decorative ambiance of the space along with the strange sculpture "beings." "The atmosphere of the restaurant is like a stage set," and to make sure that patrons sitting anywhere can enjoy the show," it can be viewed on a nine-screen video wall—raised up above eye level.

The interior is dark, as it should be in a Night Gallery. The ceiling ducts and electrical conduits are left as is and painted black—like the ceiling—so that they all disappear. The theatrical lighting is carried on a metal grid suspended down from the invisible ceiling. The dining tables are arranged on two levels: a raised platform allows for better "watching"—and for being watched. They can accommodate 200 persons and the ovular, racetrack bar can accommodate another 50 patrons. To one side is the visible kitchen and the wait station.

The exterior renovations to Night Gallery had to be approved by the Landmarks Preservation Commission. The bi-folding doors can be opened, weather permitting, to create a side walk cafe for 40 diners under the black canvas awnings. The 100 ft. long facade is eerily illuminated by the chilly blue color emanating from behind the raised black letters that spell out The Night Gallery.

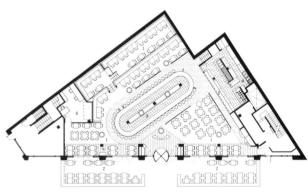

Photography:
Nathan Sayers

The designers, Engstrom Design Group, brought some of their San Francisco atmosphere along with their inspiration for the Alcatraz Brewing Co. Cafe that opened in Indianapolis. The legendary "Rock" that looms in the San Francisco Bay provided the idea for a "brewery restaurant behind bars."

Jail bars are never far from view within the Brewing Co. Raw steel bars enclose the restaurant's entrances and also appear in the booth surrounds inside. The metal railing and retail displays further the jail imagery. Twisted sections of chain link fencing hang over the dining seats—like remnants of an escape attempt. To commemorate the "checkered" pasts of criminals, the designers used the checkered motif to highlight the bar stools, the booth upholstery and the ceramic tiles areas of the floor. Other "old time" prison settings are recalled with the banded quarry tile and concrete floors, the catwalk to the mezzanine and the bare bulb-styled table light fixtures.

To add warmth and comfort to the otherwise whimsical setting, hand crafted touches were added. In the double height space, booth seating is covered in a soft chenille fabric with red, amber and green coloration. Wood and copper are used freely and a freestanding, painted steel drink rail is modeled after the classical art deco styling of the Gold Gate Bridge. Accenting the bar are glass tiles made from reconstructed beer bottles.

The Alcatraz Brewing operation is in full view of the patrons. A large, functioning grain silo—modeled after the water tower of the real Alcatraz—stands atop a steel platform above the exterior entrance. Inside, lining the mezzanine are copper and stainless steel fermenting and brewing tanks. Another row of tanks is lined up behind the bar—ready to provide the desired brew.

Gordon Biersch Brewery/Cafe
San Francisco, CA

Design:
Allied Architecture & Design and I.O.O.A.

Located in the historic Hills Bros. Coffee building on the water-front—at the foot of Bay Bridge in San Francisco—is the 16,000 sq. ft. flagship Gordon Biersch Brewery/Cafe.

The new elements in the space "have the material presence to measure up against the strength of the brick and concrete of the existing building while acting to soften and expand the palette at the same time." The designers introduced the mahogany and granite bar, the wood floor and ceiling in the dining area, the stainless steel hops tanks of the brewery and the blackened metal that runs throughout the project as "counterpoints to the existing building, adding sophistication, balance and complexity." "We wanted the space (of exposed beams and brickwork) left raw so we could incorporate some of these gutsy materials and finishes," said Roddy Creedon of Allied Architecture & Design.

The first floor bar and the second level dining areas are oriented towards the large arched windows and the spectacular bay presence beyond. On the first level, besides the bar, the brewery and the kitchen, there is a 40-seat cafe area. Since there are only ten ft. of height to the underside of the slab above, the designers cut out a section of the ceiling and opened up the dining area above for viewing from below. The walls and columns are finished with cement plaster which complements the exposed birch areas and the finish

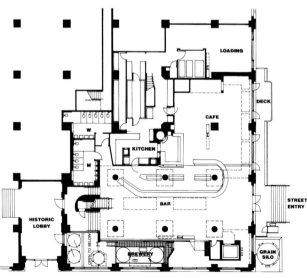

of the mahogany millwork. The workings of the brewery are revealed to the bar and beer connoisseurs who collect at the bar or in the cafe around the bar.

A stairway leads to the upper level and the 180-seat dining room. Here, too, there is a mix of textures and styles. Chairs and banquettes provide seating at the mahogany topped tables under the exposed beamed ceiling. Blackened metal railings accent the area and two-story high, stainless steel brewing tanks loom up in the background.

Through the cut-out in the floor, diners upstairs can also enjoy watching the workings of the brewing operation. Industrial-type lighting goes with the warehouse/brewery atmosphere and also provides a pleasant dining ambience.

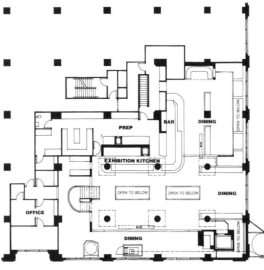

Project Team:
Roddy Creedon, Scott Williams, Lorin Hill, Douglas Burnham, Jane Chun, Tim Contreras, Grog Ensslen, Karen Mar, Neil O'Shea, Gabriel Smith and I.O.O.A.

Photography:
Richard Barnes

This, the fourth Gordon Biersch Brewery, is located in Old Town Pasadena. Nestled amid a collection of old buildings and fronting on a large courtyard at the interior of the block is this 8600 sq. ft. bar/ restaurant. The bar and dining area is entered through an oversized mahogany storefront with a raised deck covered by a curved canopy of steel and translucent panels. "The combined strength and elegance of these materials characterizes the design throughout."

The all-important and impressive mahogany and granite topped bar, in the Pasadena location, is set under a large barrel vaulted ceiling that is oriented back to the courtyard. The brewhouse—just beyond—gleams behind a soaring steel and glass window system on one side and an intimate dining mezzanine on the other. The carpeted main dining room is articulated with a raised wood floor, a matching wood ceiling, blackened iron and copper railings, mahogany booths and dining tables—all backed and visible to the exciting exhibition kitchen.

Mahogany is used to frame the windows and doors and to outline the brick and cement plaster walls. Stained concrete floors are laid in the bar and brewing areas where the stainless steel vats glisten, gleam, and brew up a source of entertainment.

Design Team:
Tim Contreras, Roddy Creedon, Jack Russ

Photography:
Allied Architecture & Design

Tib's Fleamarket & Roadhouse
Destin, FL

Design:
Zakaspace
Ft. Lauderdale, FL

It seems that retail and dining have found a common meeting place and bond in theme restaurant design. Whether it is Planet Hollywood, Hard Rock Cafe, Dick Clark's American Bandstand, or even a neon illuminated Galaxy Diner in Arizona, the sales of tee shirts, embroidered caps, coffee mugs and other "branded" souvenirs appear up front and as part of the pizzazz of the dining experience. So what is more natural than for Tib's Thibodeaux, a fictional retailer specializing in flea market merchandise, to become a restauranteur especially when his wife Marie (also part of the fiction) cooks up great red beans, gumbo and etouffe on the stove in the back room and fills the store with savory smells. So—as the story devised by Spiro Zakas and his design staff—Tibs and Marie "packed up what was left from their flea market and their pots and pans and moved to Destin (Florida) where it is said Tibs—or one of his family—is always there cooking up gumbo or playing' the cajun music."

The 10,000 sq. ft. facility designed by Zakaspace of Fort Lauderdale, overlooks a four acre lake. The "roadhouse" can seat 350 in several intimate dining spaces and the bar and lounge has additional seating on "the back porch." All the rooms are decorated with items from "the old family flea market business." The unique crafts and collectibles also serve as the background for the Cajun style live entertainment and provide the ambience for the freshly prepared, Southern Louisiana style seafood, salads, sandwiches and homemade Bayou County specialties.

Project Designer:
Spiros Zakas

Project Director:
Karen Hanlon

Photographer:
Larry Falke

The diner can entertain him or herself with a visit to the adjacent Flea Market retail space and browse the crafts, antiques, collectibles and the regional Louisiana food products or purchase the prepared dishes served in the roadhouse.

Design:
Judd Brown Designs, Inc.
Warwick, RI

A "ground-up" project, the Daily Planet is a truly American diner located off the exit from the Taconic Parkway in Poughkeepsie, NY. The Judd Brown Design firm used classic diner design elements and materials to create the original design. Starting at the standing seam, cobalt blue roof and working down to the mottled mosaic tile face, "the combination of colors, lines and scale give one an instant impression of fun and surprise within." The signage and graphics are combined with an overscaled globe clock set front and center on the facade.

The designers tell a "story" spanning the vestibule walls of the interior which is the history of the concept of diners. The interior itself is composed of tile, granite, metal and frosted glass, and a palette of clear tones of blue, bright yellows and white—underscored with accents of teal and peach. The graphics add to the "Surprise and fun" of the Daily Planet. A large metal "world" is wrapped in words proclaiming "Eating is Believing." The bakery is delineated by the large revolving cupcake. "The elements are enhanced by nostalgic media moments throughout and artifacts from different eras in American history."

The patterned mosaic tile floors and kick plates contrast with the warm wood facing of the counter, the wainscoting, and the backs of the vinyl upholstered booths. Graphics create border designs within the cut-out ceiling shapes and the designers play the blues with the teals for interest. The menu is based on classic American fare and the on-premises bakery provides fresh breads, pastries and pies.

Graphics & Signage:
Gloede Signs

Artwork:
Corporate Art Group

Photography:
Warren Jagger

Galaxy Diner
Rte 66, Flagstaff, AZ

Design Concept: Creative Team:
Summit Family Restaurants
Salt Lake City, UT
Jody Bates & Gary Bales

When traveling on Rte. 66—through Flagstaff—you'll get your kicks at the Galaxy Diner sitting alongside the road. Like a trip back in time—back to the '50s—the glittering and shimmering stainless steel, aluminum, glass block and multi-colored neon wreathed diner looks untainted, unscathed and untouched by time. Pass through the double doors under the revolving red, yellow and blue neon Galaxy logo and enter into the world of rock 'n' roll, jitterbugging, black and white movies, the TV of Leave It To Beaver—and great, home cooked food.

A giant Wurlitzer jukebox and neon stars in the ceiling set the mood in the entry as do the collection of framed old movie posters and local memorabilia in the waiting area. One is immediately aware of the music that fills the air: the music and recording artists of the '50s and '60s. The interior features two distinct dining area. One is centered around a '50s soda fountain with black, white and red tiles set and patterned around the counter, the stainless steel trim, faux marble top, mirrors and authentic looking bar stools around the circumference.

On the floor red and cream colored "linoleum" tiles make an unusual checkerboard design—interrupted by occasional black tiles. The other area—more family-oriented—has red vinyl covered mahogany colored chairs and booths and cream laminate topped tables set out on a colorful star splattered carpet.

Hanging down from the ceiling are "galaxy" inspired globe lights that recall the period and the nation's interest in Space. Train diner style windows line two sides of the restaurant.

The red, black, cream and white color scheme and the checkerboard motif are consistent throughout. No detail is too small not to have been designed and coordinated to make the "diner" period perfect.

From the crockery to the bands around the napkins to the specially-designed server's outfits—they are of a time, a place and of the color scheme. The employees wear red and white bowling shirts, poodle skirts for the women and even a custom "soda jerk" outfit for the counterperson. Many of these "uniform" elements are available for sale along with Galaxy-emblazoned souvenirs at the front end of the central counter.

The menu copy and entree names are "an integral part of the restaurant design that reflect the fun and personality associated with the '50s." One can order Blue Plate Specials served on plates with blue stars, Route 66 Pile-up appetizers, Hollywood Blvd. Brownie Sundaes, and Chubby Checker Double Decker Combos.

The Flagstaff Galaxy Diner is the fourth in the chain of these Summit Family Restaurants with 25 more planned for the next year or two. At least four or five will be in Phoenix—the rest spread out over the western states.

Design Firm:
*Design Development,
Tarzana, CA*

Photography:
Grant Heaton

Airstream Roadside Cafe
Avon, CT

Design:
Judd Brown Designs, Inc.
Warwick, RI

You can see the entire United States and never leave the charm and comfort of Avon, CT. The diner is invited to take an informal and fun-filled tour by just stepping off the dual highway that is simulated on the floor up front and enter into the imaginative wonders of Airstream Roadside Cafe. At the entrance there is a giant roadside billboard illuminating a scene of a super-highway while the scraggly grass around its base is ornamented with odd hub caps. In addition there is a piece "architecture" that suggests the garish, neon infested roadside motels circa 1950 and over the entrance a sign that indicates that the diner has arrived at the City Limits of "Airstream."

The first dining area, appropriately enough, has the look, feel, and smell—as well as color—of the roadside diners that still exist off the main highways that criss-cross the country. There are high backed, camel colored, naugahyde covered booths, a white tiled floor and black and white checkered seats pulled up to the gray linoleum topped tables. Red, yellow, and blue accents are added to brighten up the fun space.

Next on the "gastronomic tour" is a visit to Sun Valley ski resorts where amidst snowflakes on the sky blue ceiling and the snow white vinyl floor beneath, the diner can enjoy the old-fashioned travel posters and snow and ski memorabilia that has been crammed into this space along with the tables and chairs. For a change of scenery and climate—the diner can indulge in the warmth and charm of the vineyards of the Nappa Valley where a grape draped pergola becomes the focal object of the space. The final leg of the trip is back to the East Coast and up to Cape Cod with the decorative emphasis on lobster pots, fish nets, sea-faring objects and artifacts, weathered woods and shingles, captain's chairs and even a pair of anglers dangling up-side down overhead in an upturned boat.

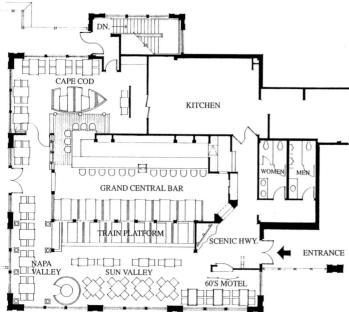

The Grand Central Bar recalls the elegance and style that was once associated with rail travel—when it was the gracious way to go.

The long, narrow space looks like the old-fashioned Pullman cars with the antimacassared red banquettes, the lowered ceiling and the "faded rug" and brass stanchions that separate the seating area from the long mahogany bar with a terrazzo cuff that matches the black and white checkered terrazzo floor. Through the "windows" the diner can enjoy the "sights" of the Sun Valley area which is adjacent to the Grand Central Bar.

It is all aboard—gas up and tank up—for a truly unique dining adventure on the go.

Project Team:
Michael Gilespie, Steven McMahon, Mark Palazio, Lisa Simeone

Photography:
Warren Jagger

Silver Max's
San Jose, CA

Design:
Backen Arrigoni & Ross
San Francisco, CA

Located in the new Pavilion Center in San Jose is Silver Max's—a "diner" based on the design spirit of the 1930s—the "era of movement." The flowing, repetitive patterns of the slick metallic motifs and accents are "symbols of the constructive period of the industrial revolution." To suggest the feeling of being continuously-on-the-go, the designers added the dynamic lines of metal and neon.

There are the sweeping, undulating curves of the fascia that wells in and out over the counter and prep area, the metal wrapped surfaces and the solitary metal clad column that nestles into the arced corner of the counter.

The same symbolism appears in the curved laminated counter tops, the crisp lighting and the floor pattern of black and white terrazzo-like floor that resembles a "machinelike grid." The color scheme is basically black, metallic silver and white with red upholstered seats and bar stools—and graphics that add to the area's sparkle and the total design impact. The "streamlined designs allow the diners to enjoy the aesthetics of the establishment while at the same time keeping up with their busy schedules."

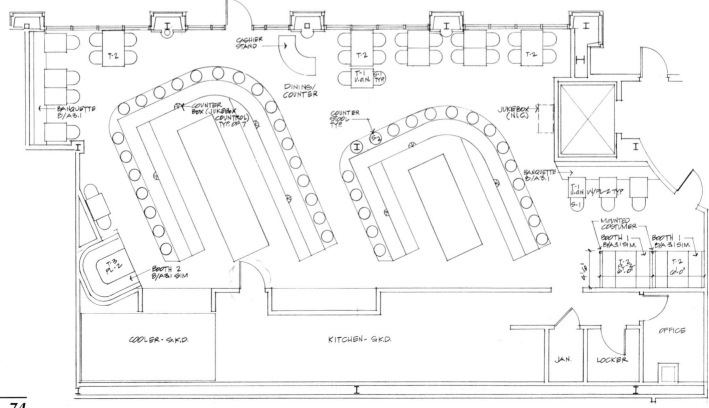

FUDGE BIG BANANA

SMOKEY RIBS CHEESE CAKE MACAROONS

PEPSI·COLA

Photography:
Don Corning

Silver Diner
Fair Oaks, Fairfax, VA

Design:
Desgrippes Gobé
New York, NY

In keeping with Robert Giaimo's desire to bring "healthy, home-style menus that incorporate the traditional diner fare with innovative new offerings that appeal to broader tastes," this—the latest in the Silver Diner chain—opened in Fairfax Co., VA. The new prototype design by Desgrippes Gobé of New York, combines "the best of the old with the best of the new."

The 240-seat diner combines classic diner design elements such as polished, stainless steel, glass blocks, and neon lighting. It also introduces state-of-the-art lighting, sound control and new architectural elements along with an updated menu. The more sophisticated interior retains the intimacy and excitement of traditional diners but with an updated color scheme, greater warmth and with lighting more sensitive to the patron's needs. Efforts were made to minimize excessive noise in the diner. The diner also retains its signature counter top and booth service, and there are individually-controlled, beautifully-refurbished, original 1940s Seeburg juke boxes at each booth and table.

On the exterior, the designers introduced an eye-catching marquee-style tower and reeded glass which mimics the lines of corrugated steel and echoes the feeling and light enhancing properties of glass block which often appeared on diners of the '50s and '60s. The bright red and silver complement the look and the materials.

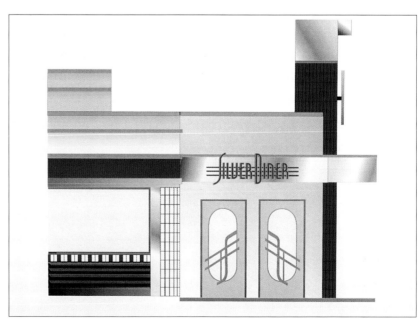

The designers of Design Collective of Columbus took what was originally a 6000 sq. ft. open dining room of a former motor lodge and redesigned it into five dining rooms. The total seating capacity of 200 is divided amongst The Diner, The Raw Bar, The Casual Dining Room, and The Formal Dining Room, and an additional 120 patrons can be seated in the Patio.

The original shell was repainted a taupe color "to allow new materials and finishes to contrast and be more visible." The "broken dish" door design is composed of discontinued quarry tiles found locally and a tile artisan shattered the tiles and arranged them in a mosaic style pattern over the major parts of the service floor and the bar. Duck cloth, gusseted and applied to the existing fireplace wall created a trompe l'oeil finish. To emulate the American Diner "dinette" furniture, the designers selected four different chair designs that are used throughout the dining room, and birch veneered plywood—stained amber, pistachio and ebony—was used for the baquettes. They "loosely depict a city skyline." Neon signs, collected from all over, were installed in the high vertical parts of the room.

In the bar of the diner zone, quilted stainless steel panels are used on the walls and the reflection of the neon and accent lights off the facetted surface creates a feeling of energy and excitement. Adding to the sparkle are accents of stainless steel and chrome: they also refer back to diner architecture. The underside of the bar continues the use of the pistachio colored birch veneered plywood and the bar stools, in two sizes, are covered in persimmon, gold, purple and black. They are used randomly to stress the informal, casual style of the restaurant.

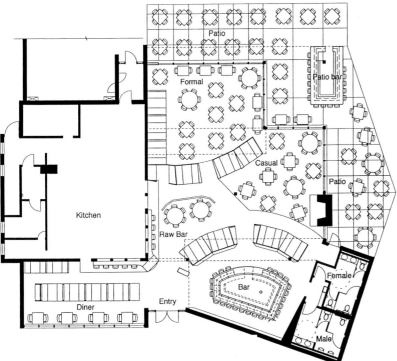

The main dining room floor is covered with a multi-thread nylon carpet and appearing on it are high gloss, black laminated tables edged with stainless steel—to recreate the dinette furniture of the '50s and '60s. The Italian light fixtures are suspended at assorted heights—like stars in the sky.

Photography:
StudiOhio

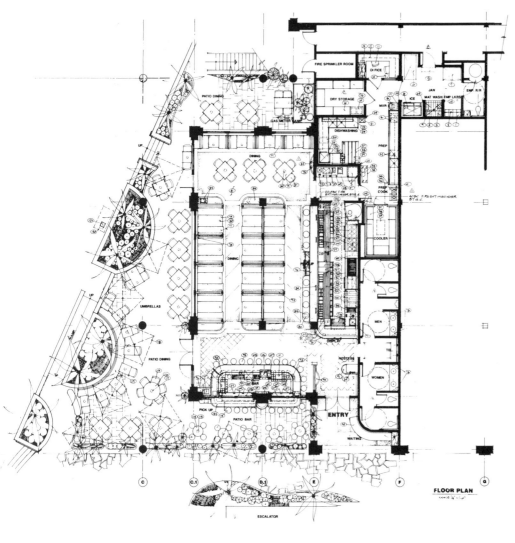

The streamlined mass of chrome, assembled in a manner reflective of the diners of the 1950s, is perched along the waterfront of downtown Honolulu. Scott's Grill & Bar, designed by Hatch Design Group of Costa Mesa, CA, follows the classic diner style with a layout that consists of counter and booth dining areas with additional space allotted for a lounge and patio.

The 5900 sq. ft. space is casual and yet refined, and it appeals to both tourists and local business people. The black vinyl linoleum counter tops are edged with ribbed steel bands, and the black contrasts dramatically with the white crockery. The black and white palette is repeated on the diamond checkerboard patterned floor.

The bar stools are upholstered in cream vinyl while the booth seating combines the cream vinyl with welting and bands of persimmon red. Birch wood and mahogany are used throughout—often together for color and contrast. The booth ends utilize the two woods decoratively while mahogany veneer is used to cover the structural columns.

There are windows on three sides and during the day the space is filled with natural light. "The front window is an exaggerated radius to take advantage of the view and the doors have radius tops and bottoms to strengthen the diner-like appearance of the restaurant," said Jeff Hatch, the designer. At night, computer controlled low voltage lighting is provided. The coffered ceiling from which the steel and milk glass pendant fixtures hang is finished in mahogany and painted wood, and like the doors and windows—the coffers have radius ends.

The busy and action filled kitchen is located just behind the counter dining area. The counter top is zinc, and steel desk lamps on the counter tops act as a "visual barrier" between the patrons and the cooks. Facing the entrance and at the rounded end of the counter is a glass-enclosed seafood display case. It colorfully tells incoming diners what is fresh—and what's available. "The result is a dynamic, inviting eatery that is reminiscent of the past yet appealing to patrons of today."

Design Team:
Jeff Hatch, Bruce Bentley, Jackie Hanson, Todd Hatch, Donna Kruse, Ben Pollock, Diane Varney

Photography:
Anderson, Greenbrea, CA

Shake Burger and Roll
Ardmore, PA

Design:
Hugh Boyd, Boyd Assoc.
Montclair, NJ

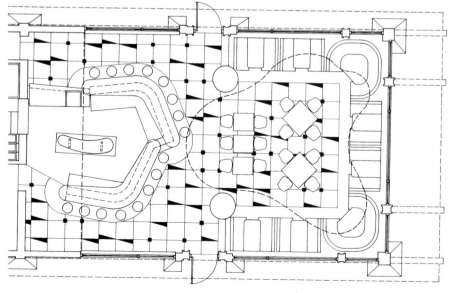

The designer describes the 1768 sq. ft. burger/ice-cream "joint" as "The Jetsons meet Elsie the Cow." The "joint" has a '50s Jetson feeling combined with a very '90s tempo. The promoters wanted a '50s-style "hangout" complete with '50s and '60s music recreated in a vacant Roy Rogers space, and since the budget was very limited, the designer worked with paint, plastic laminates, linoleum on the floor—and lots of panache.

The two critical markets needed to make the space work are the young children and their mothers who come for lunch or after school snacks and the college students for the evening hour trade. The designer picked the Jetson cartoon series as the design concept since it was so filled with images and shapes that were popular in the '50-'60s— and they are still around today.

The counter tops and table tops combine the irregular shapes and angular forms to resemble "cowskin" and the funnel shaped columns that support the amoeba shaped dropped ceiling look like something that has been cleaned up and transported from Flintrock. Here tungsten bulbs sparkle through the openings in the floating, edge-lit shape. This is what attracts the passersby who can see in through the wide open glass windows that surround the space. The columns also serve to frame the focal point of the design—the boomerang-shaped soda fountain with its neon-lit, "rock" shaped mirrors and corrugated fins— backed up with natural plywood storage cabinets above.

The color scheme is quite neutral; in addition to the black and white the scheme includes camel colored naugahyde upholstery on bar stools and on the booths that hug the window line. The floor is laid with beige and camel linoleum squares accented with black and the major accent colors are the soft teal of the columns and the floating ceiling and the marigold yellow that appears on the convoluted valence above the windows in the rear and on the squares appliqued onto the wall behind the soda fountain counter.

Design:
FRCH Worldwide Design
Cincinnati, OH

Jeepers!, 26,000 sq. ft. facility opened in Rockville, MD—just a few miles outside of Washington, DC. It is a prototype designed by the FRCH Worldwide Design firm for Jungle Jim Playlands, Inc. and already the client is rolling out replicas in various other locations. The family entertainment center is a mini-theme park for children 2 to 12, and it includes a Pizza Hut food service in the Tiny Rhino Diner which as a 1950's design and a child-oriented, "happy food" menu. Jeepers! also has facilities for catering private parties, for soft play dates, or for just places for kids to enjoy themselves. There is a staging area for live entertainment where the "characters" that inhabit Jeepers! can put on magic acts, puppet shows or audience participation shows.

Working within a limited budget, the design firm opted for a graphics based solution that relies heavily on elaborate theming. "Bold colors, whacky shapes, startling textures, vivid patterns, theatrical lighting and jungle imagery" were used in high-contrast combinations to create a feeling of energy and excitement. The designers also created a family of characters: (J.J. the monkey, his pal Kronkle and Trish the Tiny Rhino after whom the diner is named. Actors, dressed up as the characters interact with the children as well as perform on the treehouse-like stage.

Relatively inexpensive materials such as painted gypsum wall board and stained strand board were used and the resources were concentrated on the strategically placed focal points.

Special attention was given to the elaborate portals in front of the rides "to heighten the excitement and establish a distinct identity."

The concept has proven so successful that the design firm is now developing a "scaled down" version—Jeepers Jr! that will open in some select Toys 'R' Us Kid's World stores. The employees' outfits were designed to complement the theme and a whole line of collateral branded merchandise (stuffed animals, tee shirts, sweats, caps, mugs, etc.) is also available in Jeepers!

Team Director:
Michael Beechly

Photographer:
George Cott, Chroma Inc.,
Tampa, FL

Design Concept:
Bobby Moore, Orlando, FL

When fans of the fastest growing viewer sport in the world can indulge their fantasies of high speed racing and life threatening drag races with fun food in an exciting setting—then a true theme restaurant has been waved past the finish line. Race Rock in "ga-ga-land Orlando" is a 20,000 sq. ft., full service restaurant which also happens to feature one of the most extensive collections of authentic racing memorabilia. At Race Rock tribute is paid to all racing from NASCAR's and Indy cars to dragsters and speedboats with displays and exhibits from the greatest races and racers of all time.

Bobby Moore, a restauranteur and racing enthusiast, brought together some of the biggest names in racing to open Race Rock, and they also provided some of the unique, one-of-a-kind props that make the ambience of this theme restaurant so special.

In addition to the 1989 Lola Indy car driven by the Andretti's, the drag racing "funny car" of John Forces, a Top Fuel dragster, a monster truck and drag bike as well as floating hydroplanes. There is a multi-screen video system that provides diners with thrilling, death-defying and hilarious moments of the assorted racing sports. This puts the diner in the driver's seat.

Photography:
Robert Starling
Photography, Orlando, FL

The black and white checkered pattern, so identified with racing flags, dominates the palette of the space and its graphics. Complementing that motif are primary colored accents and the sleek, silvery sheen of metallics.

The fun and fancy continues in the "racing menu" where appetizers are listed under "Start Your Engine," "Circle Traces" are pizzas, and "Pole Position Pastas" come before "The Main Event." Of course, the desserts are collected under "The Victory Lap." The checkered pattern and bright yellow of the menu add a festive feeling to the table setting. As the reader may have discovered in so many of the Theme Restaurants gathered in this book—here, too, the souvenir shop is alive and doing well. It is well stocked with licensed merchandise, license plates, tattoes, mugs, caps and even authentic collectibles.

Don't be surprised to see a new Race Rock checkered roof and speed racer zooming at you very soon in Las Vegas, New York, London and Tokyo.

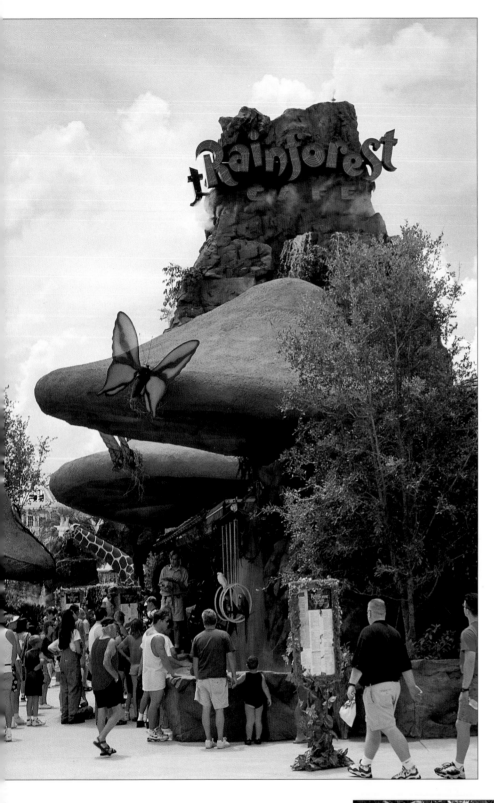

Rainforest Cafe, located in the already magical kingdom of Disneyland, adds new wonders upon wonders. It is a dynamic restaurant/retail environment that recreates the feeling of a tropical rainforest—and the inhabitants thereof.

"Imagine a tropical wonderland with cool mists that permeate through cascading waterfalls; crescendos of thunder and lighting; continuous tropical rainstorms; huge mushroom canopies; animation featuring Tracy the Talking Tree, whimsical butterflies, crocodiles, snakes and frogs, trumpeting elephants and entertaining gorillas; all moving within the surroundings of larger than life banyan trees with the sounds and aromas of a tropical rainforest"— plus great, imaginative and popularly-priced foods to delight the whole family.

The brainchild of Steve Schussler, the first Rainforest Cafe opened only a year or so ago in a 13,850 sq. ft. space in the Mall of America, and the concept is already "on the road" and rapidly spreading into other parts of the country. "Rainforest Cafe started with my love for animals. I was looking for an environment for my tropical birds—something that would make them comfortable," said Steve Schussler about the concept which had been brewing for over ten years.

Rainforest Cafe

It is a draw as to which is the greater attraction: the food and drinks served in the make-believe, larger than life "rainforest," or the retail space filled with colorful and lovable "branded" tee shirts, sweats, caps, stuffed animals and toys. There is even a pet shop where a shopper can purchase an exotic toucan, macaw or cockatoo.

However, the main thrust is the rainforest theme that has been inspired by and designed to respect the environment and the natural world. It is an ecologists fondest dream come true.

In creating this fantasy, the designer/conceptualist Steve Schussler working with design firms such as Shea Architects and Jon Greenberg Assoc., has fashioned a giant 38 ft. diameter "mushroom" that caps the Magic Mushroom Juice Bar which is equipped with amusing animal- and bird-legged bar stools; dolphins that appear to leap through the 12 ft. high waterfalls that operate on a recirculating pump with a sophisticated filtration system that ensures clear, clean water without waste; a mechanical snake slithers about over concrete "rocks"; a snapping crocodile in a pond—and every step and every turn presents a new sight and introduces a new adventure.

The concrete floor has been treated with tinted muriatic acid to simulate the multi-colored, "muddy" floors of the rainforest. Giant fresh water aquariums appear as part of the cash wrap desk in the retail section, and they form an arch at the restaurant's entrance.

Additional tanks are used in the restaurant and they are stocked with over 130 varieties of fresh and salt water fish. Hand made, synthetic "coral reefs" provide the ambience in the tanks and they were designed so as not to disturb the delicate balance of the tanks and salt water ecosystem.

A full-time curator and a staff of animal care specialists care for the aquariums and the exotic birds that are on display, and they are on hand to share their knowledge and answer questions. Though most of the "Rainforest's" foliage is artificial, live Bromeliads and other low light plants are integrated into the "plantings."

The rate at which Rainforest Cafes is spreading to other parts of the country—from California to Las Vegas to Denver to Florida to New York—is unbelievable but a success breeds success and the theme restaurant/retail complex is bringing in the crowds. Also on the board are Rainforest Cafes for Cancun, Mexico and London, England.

Design:
*Conceptual & Interior
Design: Steve Schussler*

Consultant Designers:
*Shea Architects,
Minneapolis, MN
Jon Greenberg Assoc.,
Southfield, MI*

Photography:
*Bob Perzel, Perzel
Photography Group*

93

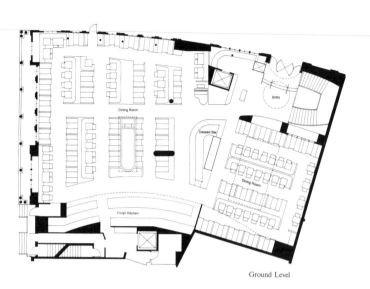

Ground Level

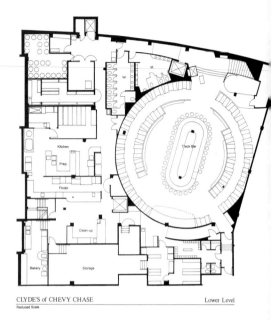

CLYDE'S of CHEVY CHASE
Reduced Scale
Lower Level

Clyde's embodies the fun and fantasy of the luxury travel and the places to travel. The theme restaurant takes its patrons on a world wide jaunt traveling in the style of the luxurious '20s up through the fabled '50s. The 17,500 sq. ft. offers many different venues to challenge the patrons imagination on the two levels.

It starts in the large, skylit foyer with the radiating patterned terrazzo floor. The flush anigre paneled walls recall the handsome art deco styled liners of the '30s, and on the raised wall block steamer trunks, valises and boxes are stacked ready to be loaded on board for the voyage. The largest of the dining rooms lies beyond and the Ocean Liner theme is stated in the giant ship model center and the large model airplanes that hang from the special acoustic fabric panel ceiling.

The Dessert Bar—all copper, brass and stainless steel—is a welcome oasis between the Ocean Liner room and the next dining area. The bar is decorated with wave patterns on the face and a custom pewter bar top which is handcrafted and enhanced with an art deco edge trim.

The Oriental Express room is fashioned after the famous European luxury train of the '20s and '30s. The ribbon striped mahogany sheathed room is detailed with art deco trim. The marquetry panels and the brass wall sconces were produced by the same English firm that made the originals used on the Orient Express. Brass luggage racks, overhead, hold vintage boxes, valises and leather luggage.

A 100 ft. mural runs across the entire first floor dining space and it depicts the voyage and the stops made by the Orient Express as well as other high points in world air and ship travel. Fine arts, posters, memorabilia and ship and plane models are "tastefully displayed to add to the romance and fun of the overall image." Lighting throughout is provided by custom pendants, wall sconces and assorted track lights.

A staircase with a nautical theme leads diners past an 18 ft. square mural of a vintage car race to the Track Bar. This large circular space is ringed with perforated red leather booths designed to recall sports car upholstery. A bright red limited production Jaguar and a three wheel Morgan are "parked" near the entrance.

Two large chrome plated hood ornaments, framed in special mirror enclosures, loom over eithe end of the bar while the raised bar back supports a 1940's shiny black dirt racer. An eight ft. high by 120 ft. long mural depicts the evolution of sports cars from the 1920s to the 1950s.

Rare automobile posters grace a dark green wall. The ceiling of the Track Bar is exposed concrete painted charcoal with metal acoustic panels between the ribs and the lighting is on custom radiused tracks.

Architect:
Leon Chatelain III and John Richards Andrews,

Photography:
Ron Blunt Photography, Alexandria, VA

"An American legendary style was the main driving force of the design of the Harley Davidson Cafe in New York City," says Tommy Chi, the designer of the 12,000 sq. ft. restaurant/cafe divided between two levels in a midtown New York building.

The design team has melded nostalgia and modern elements together by the use of materials. "Natural timber contrasts with metal and the movement of lighting to give the patrons a sensation of passing through a time zone of the American legend." The cafe design is all American and patriotic. A map of the U.S. is stencil cut into the underside of the building's existing canopy and twin-V Harley Davidsons signature engines introduce the light sconces that anchor the perimeter of the steel facade. According to the design firm, Harley Davidson symbolizes an era of rock and roll, movies, sports and wars fought

throughout the last 90 years, and they have crammed as much of that imagery into the design with artwork, artifacts, graphics and photographs.

The bar area has an 18 ft. coffered ceiling over it. Immediately over the bar is mounted the first Harley Davidson motorcycle. Other HD motorcycles—many previously owned by celebrities—are displayed on a catwalk constructed of vertical and horizontal I-beams and metal grids. This metal catwalk delineates the bar area, the retail shop and the main dining room. Smoke machines and strobe lights, attached to the catwalk, provide "additional visual energy."

The main dining room is dominated by a prefabricated metal panel which unfurls overhead as a free floating American flag. It serves as a second ceiling and envelops diners in a "totally made-in-American feeling."

Elvis Presley posters cover a whole wall in the main dining room and next to the bar to integrate "rock and roll" with the Harley Davidson history. Throughout the ground level, the lighting is "dramatic and sparkly" and focused primarily on the visual elements on the catwalk and ceiling. The ambient light is secondary, almost completely-reflected light.

The entire basement level is superimposed by images of the famous American highway Route 66, and different cement adhesive textures combined with stainless steel indicate noteworthy American points of interest.

Photographer:
Norman McGrath

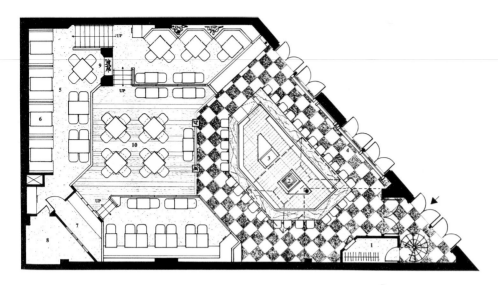

Located in Greenwich Village where it is surrounded by other restaurants that also cater to "Village" tourists and weekend singles, the Garage Cafe has gone back to its roots. The 100 year old red brick building was originally a garage and also—somewhere in its past—a theater in the round. Rather than play up autos or auto parts for theme, the designers, Elias Design Group, opted to "suggest the building's origins in an abstract way." Though the owner requested that the Garage be fresh and new, he also wanted the warmth and charm that are inherent in so many of the older eating establishments in the village.

The 3000 sq. ft. space was stripped back to its original brick wall and wood timbered ceiling. Seating was designed on four rising levels so that the activity in the open kitchen and on the

Design Team:
Brad Elias, David Snyder
Photography:
Peter Paige, New York, NY

dance floor can be viewed and enjoyed from almost every seat. The design also puts intimate dining, the manager's office and the D.J.'s booth over the kitchen and restrooms.

A very trendy bar is located along the Seventh Ave. storefront and there is a visible burger grill station within the bar. An oversized copper hood over the bar not only provides ducting for the burger grill but it serves for liquor storage and as an emphatic canopy over the bar.

The "mood" changes as one steps further into the Garage: the space takes on a more rustic, lodge-like ambience and a warmer feeling as one approaches the kitchen and the rear platform. The four-paned windows of the kitchen all open upward for the waiter service and for viewing. The working fireplace, on the rear platform, is also visible throughout. Diners can sit at the bar or at tables set out on the four levels. The private booths on the upper level are equipped with individual lighting dimmers so the diners can control their own environment.

Auto parts metal sculptures by Kamakasi and Mark Dornan's carved wooden sculptures of tools and dining utensils are located between the bar and the dining spaces "to further reinforce the fusion of styles." A slightly misshapen chandelier is centered over the main dining/dancing area to "vertically dimension the space." Between the bar and dining areas, 115 patrons can be seated with an additional 40 seats, weather permitting, in the outdoor cafe.

Design Team:
Brad Elias, David Snyder
Photography:
Peter Paige, New York, NY

Flat Pennies
Denver, CO

Design:
Semple Brown Roberts
Denver, CO

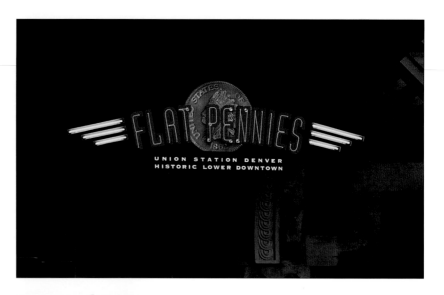

The design concept for Flat Pennies, located in a 2800 sq. ft. space in the 1870 Union Station in the historic district of lower Downtown Denver, was to maintain the original use and spirit of the place. Thus, railroads and trains are represented "in elegant, contrasting and sometimes whimsical details."

The space is organized with a central bar, booths to one side and a mezzanine on the opposite side, and tables spaced all around. A mezzanine was created over the kitchen which breaks the voluminous scale of the 20 ft. ceilings and it also serves as a two-story backdrop to the restaurant. To further create a more intimate feeling, a canopy is suspended over the bar and there are four foot wide pendant light fixtures dropped from the ceiling. The lamp posts, at the booths, are at an intermediary height of 10 ft.

Borrowed interpretations of the original restaurant design are the black and white tile floor around the bar, the central "island" dining counter and the lighting fixtures. Supporting the railroad theme, steel railroad tracks hold up the bar canopy and they are also used as bar foot rails. Crossover bridges inspired the metal and mesh stairs that lead up to the mezzanine, and even the lamp posts along "booth alley" recall the telegraph poles that once bordered the rails.

Dark blue fabric, red wood, steel and maple dominate the Flat Pennies palette and they are highlighted with pennies embedded in the booth table tops, the modernized replicas of vintage neon signs advertising Flat Pennies Beers, and a 15x15 ft. mural in bright red, blue and yellow.

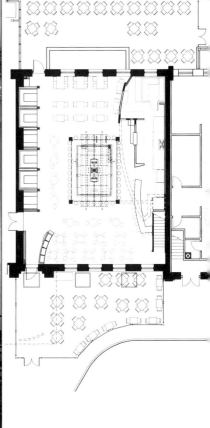

Principal in Charge:
Sarah Brown

Project Architect:
Andrew D. Moss

Design Team:
Donna Hoover, Brad Smith

Quotes: Isabelle Matteson

Signage & Graphics:
Weber Design

Photography:
Andrew Kramer, AIA, Boulder, CO

Design:
Semple Brown Roberts
Denver, CO

The 6000 sq. ft. restaurant in the historic landmark Larimer Square district "combines the obvious with the unexpected," on two levels of 3000 sq. ft. each. The architectural details of the turn-of-the-century building that is part of the space is integrated with a new and stimulating interior. The design firm, Semple Brown Roberts, was able to unite the older structure with a new addition. The red brick building now has a cornice that meets with one on an adjacent building while a pediment towers over the corner entrance. Large windows all around the building and a "New West" sign over the entrance invite patrons to enter.

"Where the exterior relates to its environment, the interior explodes with its own flavor." This is the "new west"—or at least the west of the retro '50s

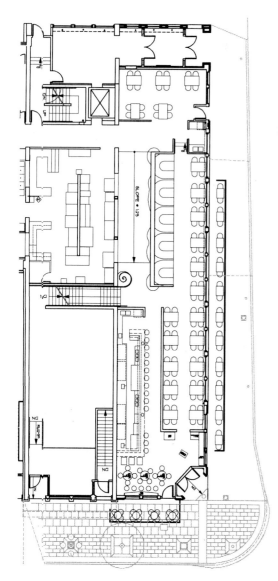

where rather than horses and saddles we have cowboys driving Cadillacs and wearing Rolex watches on their wrists instead of packing six shooters on their hips. This was the concept worked out by Sarah Brown and Randy Rutherford of The Larimer Group, the client.

Inside the space which can accommodate 225 diners, from booths to the bar, from floor to ceiling "steering wheels and cowboy boots, saddles and the nose of a Cadillac, neon lights and a Sky Chief" are used to create a memorable experience.

Inspired by the old Burma Shave signs that once graced old Rte 66, the designers have added a series of signs over the bar which is

located to the left of the entrance. Seating in the 100 ft. long space is provided at small tables along the windows on the right, and there is a series of tall back booths that form a central spine in the layout. The banquettes are upholstered in a fabric filled with the colors and shapes more reminiscent of Matisse than of the old corral. At the end of the bar are stairs that lead to the second floor patio where there is a splendid view of the Rocky Mountains and the James Dean room—a place for private parties.

Cleverly and subtly, the designers made references to diners and the American eating tradition. The design seems to appeal to the locals as well as the fun-seeking tourists to Larimer Square.

Principal in Charge:
Sarah Brown

Project Architect:
Lynne Thom

Quotes:
Isabelle Matteson

Signage & Graphics:
Weber Design

Photography:
Andrew Kramer, AIA,
Boulder, CO

From the outside, Route 66 recalls the roadside architecture found along the "mother road"— the original Rte 66: simple buildings crowned with great signs designed for the age of the automobile. The porch and raised storefront are set in front of the 1920s former auto repair garage "like a grand billboard of corrugated steel and neon." The simplicity of the design contrasts with the surrounding glitz of this strip of Sunrise Highway on Long Island.

The Pentagram design team brings back the roadhouse diner inside without overdoing the "nostalgia." The floor is striped, the upholstered banquettes are two toned and the light fixtures are fashioned out of hub caps. At the rear of the restaurant is an enormous painted wooden billboard that frames a room covered entirely with period postcards of places along the old Rte. 66. The open bar is a trellised metal frame hung with lights and rolling TVs. It is backed up by a silvery, corrugated wall. Auto body shop references are noted throughout the bar design: the corrugated steel wall, the neon clock, and the garage door tracks that support the TVs and the lights.

The wall between the dining rooms features odd size doorways and even a cowboy cut-out while a Rte. 66 "road map" covers another wall in the main dining room. Throughout, the graphics, also by Pentagram, feature the logo with the sunburst medallion and the "66."

"Route 66 is not just a place, it's a state of mind"—and this place keeps it fresh and always there.

Partner/Architect:
James Biber

Architect:
Michael Zweck Bronner

Coordinator:
Leslie Wellott

Partner/Graphics:
Michael Bierut

Graphic Designer:
Emily Hayes

Photography:
Peter Mauss/Esto

Design:
Meisel Ltd. Associates
Chicago, IL

This project is part of a new, night-time entertainment theme park called Pleasure Island which is located next to Disney world in Orlando. The area is created around the mythical misadventures of Capt. Merriweather Pleasure. "To this end, the plan of Fireworks is organized around the remains of blast bunkers built of used brick surrounding a steel and wood deck mezzanine. The detailing of the structure uses the vocabulary of open steel trusses and lattice columns to imply the archaeology of the myth. All of this culminates in the distorted ruins of the old watch-tower which becomes a 'chandelier' in the 35 ft. space."

Throughout, industrial materials are used; the floor is treated and block pine with brick pavers are utilized in the traffic areas and as a border for the black carpeted areas. Exterior grade corrugated metal walls are partially concealed by a pattern of acoustic panels covered in natural burlap and the walls have a wainscotting of black and yellow diagonally striped laminates.

A "roadhouse bar" that seas 100 is adjacent to the 300-seat, family style barbecue restaurant and here, too, the materials are "factory" related and totally eclectic.

Industrial lighting is used throughout with colored gels used to accent a collection of fireworks dummies. Neon is used for sculptural details as well as signage and as a "reminder of the mythical factory's earlier conflagration."

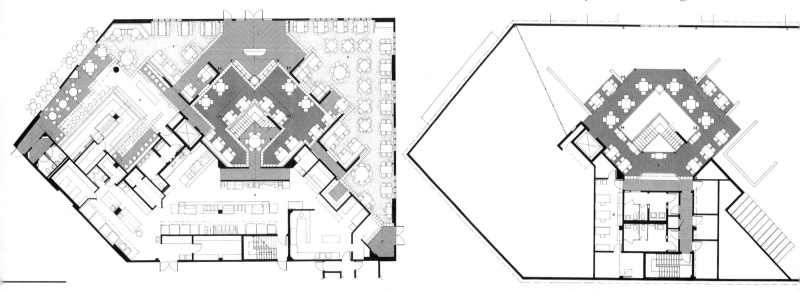

Contractor:
Capitol Construction
Group, Inc.

Photography:
Erin L. O'Brien
Photography,
Cape Canaveral, FL

Hard Rock Cafe
Myrtle Beach, SC

Design:
*Zakaspace
Ft. Lauderdale, FL*

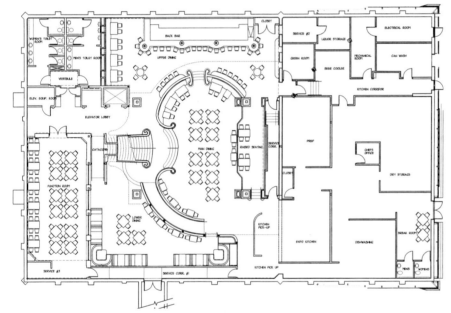

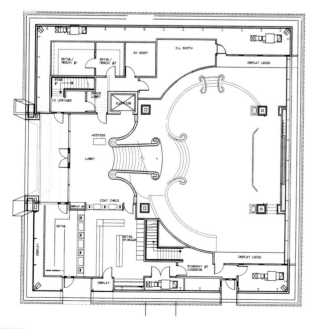

Probably the grand-daddy of the current wave of entertainment/memorabilia filled eateries is the Hard Rock Cafe, with outposts that seem to cover the world. For their recent incarnation in Myrtle Beach, the company wanted something more contemporary that "blended the Hard Rock's focus on rock 'n' roll with a classic architecture style." The design firm of Zakaspace came up with a pyramid as an icon and themed the cafe's interior and exterior with ancient Egyptian design motifs since, such as the ancient pyramids. "Rock music is timeless and has the power to transcend time, cultures and boundaries."

The 70 ft. high pyramid sits atop tiered levels of lush landscaping and cascading fountains, and the building is flanked by bronze-like sphinxes. A 25 ft. wide staircase leads up to the entrance where the visitor can view the "catacomb" styled main dining area, that seats 250 patrons, from the mezzanine.

A dramatic, wide central stairway leads down to the dining room which is actually 13 ft. below ground level. The stage, at the far end, is finished with an elaborate 14 ft. by 14 ft. stained glass back wall that features the Egyptian god of eternity. The wall shimmers in greens, blues, turquoise, magentas, reds and beige. The ceiling, in the center of the 19,000 sq. ft. pyramid structure reaches a height of 22 ft.

A 36 ft. mahogany and bird's eye maple bar is located on an intermediate platform between the entry mezzanine level and the dining room below. Overscaled, cone-shaped alabaster lighting fixtures sit on the bar and accentuate the curved bump outs that break up the length of the bar. Rich mahogany paneling is used throughout.

The large limestone bricks that cover the wall are inscribed with hieroglyphics that carry rock 'n' roll related messages as well as some Hard Rock values (Love All, Serve All). The blocks are realistically painted in colors that reflect

the warmth of the wood and stone-like floors. More hieroglyphic messages arc inscribed on the red base area of the stained glass wall: "And in the end the love you take equals the love you give"—"Take time to be kind"—"All Is One" and "Save the Planet."

The side dining room is warmer and more intimate with its lowered ceiling and carpeted floors. The booths, along the wall, are upholstered in an Egyptian themed chenille fabric and diners are given a great view of the open kitchen beyond. Also in keeping with the Egyptian theme is the mahogany paneled and warmly lit "Phunction" room.

Extensive research into ancient Egyptian architecture, building materials and hieroglyphic messages provided the foundation upon which Zakaspace created this Hard Rock Cafe—but with design liberties taken. Special attention was given to the display cases that house the all-important memorabilia.

Principal in Charge:
Spiro Zakas

Design Team:
Karen Schultz

Stained Glass:
Kebrle Stained Glass
Studio, Dallas, TX

Photography:
Colin Addis, Myrtle
Beach, SC

Under the big toque in the theater of exhibition kitchens

- *Wok Magic*

- *High Flying Pizzas*

- *Sushi Strippers & Snippers*

- *Glowing Grills & Open Hearths*

- *Center Ring Rotisseries*

- *Tables Top Tossers*

    and a supporting cast of Cuisine Artistes...

The designers of Cafe Casablanca toured the Mediterranean and North African coast and selected elements from Morocco and southern Spain which they incorporated into the restaurant's design. It is North African in concept and reminiscent of Rick's Cafe American of "Casablanca" film fame. The theme is decidedly in keeping with the overall casino concept of which this is an important part. Meals are served here all day long to a rather diverse market growth.

The major focal element of the restaurant, and thus the design, is the lavish buffet which is featured on a raised mezzanine and visually evident from all over the room. Supporting the food display is an earthy, rich, but neutral color scheme. The creamy stucco walls are interrupted by arches and by stylized Moorish latticed niches, and the cream color is highlighted and accented by borders of colorful imported Spanish and Moroccan tiles. The floors combine areas of terra cotta tiles with those of wood, and the same vibrant red/brown color coats the acoustic tile ceiling. The ceiling is segmented by the beams that emanate from the tops of the columns spaced evenly around the room. The columns also tend to divide the large space into more intimate sections.

Adding to the North African ambience are the rotating ceiling fans, the palm trees and the wood slatted shutters on the windows. There are also the kilm fabrics that upholster the booth seats and the banquettes, and the authentic Moroccan pottery and artifacts especially selected for this project.

Blues and greens, in muted faux finishes, are used on the buffet servers and the dining tables to complement the terra cotta colored floors and ceiling. The chairs of light, woven rattan provide another dollop of Moroccan intrigue to the proceedings as do the silk and bead fringed lighting fixtures dangling over the bar.

Cafe Casablanca

Of special interest are the skylights and "twig roofs" that dramatize the rear dining areas. Building on the mood and style that made Rick's Place the place to be when in Casablanca, Knauer, Inc. has devised its own variation on that theme with its romantic, mysterious and exotic ambience.

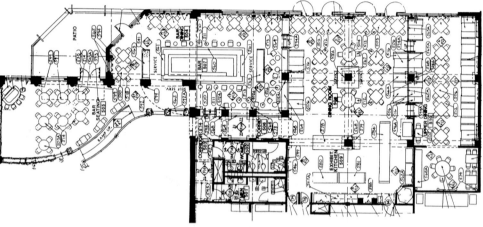

Principals:
Mark Knauer, AIA &
Danilo D. Yanong, AIA

Project Designers:
Mark Knauer, Carmen,
Polly Schwartz, David
Sanderson, Katherine
Ingrassio

Photography:
James Yochum

Described as "a Mediterranean grill for the '90s that captures the spirit of classic modernism," Spazzo is perched high up in a commercial building in Bellevue—a city just across the water from Seattle. From this lofty, window filled space, diners can look out over the serene landscape or look in towards the colorful, art filled, atmospheric and color rich interior created by Mesher Shing & Associates of Seattle. A former restaurant was metamorphosed to this fun, relaxed and theatrical dining experience by the many murals in the 10,000 sq. ft. space. The artwork was inspired by 20th century Mediterranean based painters such as Pablo Picasso, Joan Miro, Henri Matisse and Fernand Leger.

The tapes bar is the focal point with its unique, star-shaped light fixtures spiraling down from the ceiling and contrasting with the Mediterranean style iron railing below. Metal sculptures and wrought iron metal details are evident throughout and help emphasize the "spirit" of the restaurant. Iron fish serve as pedestals to support the bar.

Natural, light brown stained floors are enhanced by the deeper brown wood beams installed overhead to make the space look more like a taverna than the penthouse of a business building—that it is. In some areas, the wood floor is replaced by assorted odd shaped tiles or overlaid with oriental style runners. Antique oak credenzas lend credence to the Mediterranean attitude as they replace the usual stainless steel wait stations. The simple, mahogany colored chairs with black vinyl seats are complemented by the crisp white table linens. Guests seated at the tables or at the elevated bar can enjoy the show provided by the open kitchen and its wood fire ovens.

"The decor is layered—paint and fabric—and splattered paint is intentionally left on many light fixtures." But, where ever the eye wanders—as one exits from the elevator—searches for the right restroom—sits at the bar—it is the fabulous artwork and murals by Eclectic Surfaces that adds so much to the creative menu being served with style and panache.

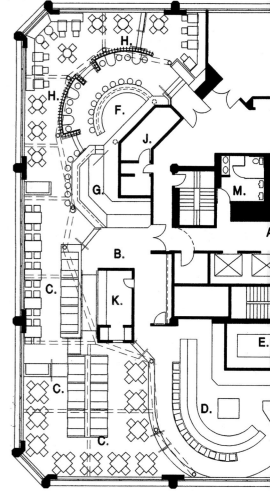

Murals:
Eclectic Surfaces,
Seattle, WA

Logo & Menu Graphics:
Tim Girvin Designs,
Seattle, WA

Faux Finishes:
Schermer Paint Co.

Specialty Metal Work:
Pacific Stainless Steel

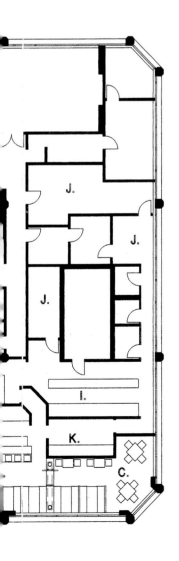

This flagship restaurant, designed by "Jack" Baum of Tree House Design, is the prototype for a chain of informal restaurants that are planned to be rolled out in North America and Europe. The owner's program required a space that was "suggestive of a long-established and somewhat worn, country or coastal cafe that one might find anywhere along the Mediterranean coast." The space also had to be warm and inviting-casual and bright-and be suited to settings like at Cocowalk which is an open air mall.

The design program called for an open kitchen, a wood burning pizza oven, and a holding bar that would also act as a serving bar. With these requirements, Baum tried to affect the ambience of a remote country market where the food display and preparation

Overhead the ceiling is a mixture of rough hewn timber construction and stucco with custom, cone-shaped, pendant lighting fixtures of galvanized zinc. The perimeter lights are recessed with rings of colored, Italian Murano glass. The floor has a border of pre-cast "keystone" concrete tiles, like those used on the exterior plaza, and a field of handmade, terra cotta tiles accented with occasion decorative, glazed tiles. Around the perimeter of the space is "a custom painted wood store front with stained glass accents that opens up to extend the restaurant out into the exterior plaza" where there is another 500 sq. ft. of seating area.

In addition, there is a 1000 sq. ft. free-standing, self-service-take-out outlet that is similar in style to the cafe which also faces the exterior courtyard.

Designer:
Julius S. "Jack" Baum

Design Team:
Karen Tappis, Greg Harry

Architect:
M.C. Harry &
Associates, Miami, FL

Photography:
Karl Francetic,
New Medford, CT

would be the main focus and the seating area would be like that of an outdoor cafe alongside the market. The 5000 sq. ft. space is divided into two by the central "street" which is actually a continuation of the open air arcade of the exterior of the Cafe Med. At one end of the "street" one can see the open kitchen and the pizza oven where the hood over the kitchen is made of oxidized and polished zinc. The same finishes are used on the bar which is to the right of the kitchen. A lattice grill acts as a cage to lock up the back bar after closing but during the open hours it is hooked to the ceiling and creates an awning-like element over the back bar. On the opposite side of the "street" is the seating area with the table tops stained deep green and accented with decorative tiles.

Evvia Estiatorio
Palo Alto, CA

Design:
Backen Arrigoni Ross, Architects
San Francisco, CA

The unusual restaurant, located in the historic downtown district of Palo Alto, combines elements of a rustic Greek taverna with the casual indoor-outdoor California aesthetic. The 2000 sq. ft. space, originally a high-tech, Italian restaurant, was converted by the design firm of Backen Arrigoni Ross of San Francisco by reconfiguring the space so that the preparation and cooking of the food is part of the dining room design.

The dining area is anchored by a four ft. by 16 ft. antique wood dining table centrally located under a skylight. On one side is the large brick and plaster fireplace and flanking the table on the other side is the "forno": the woodburning, Greek oven and rotisserie/grill. The rear wall is a glowing display "pantry wall" which is highlighted by back-lit niches containing bottles and jars of infused olive oils, vinegars and marinated vegetables.

The rustic atmosphere is emphasized by the use of antique pine for the furniture and the fixtures, the warm glow cast by the amber glass shades on the custom table lamps and candlesticks, the exuberant display of Greek terra cotta pottery and ceramics, the antique copper pots and pans, and the hand-forged wrought iron that appears throughout the space. To create intimate seating areas within the dining room, the designers added the traditional feature of Greek cafes—barrels of wine stacked up on low platforms that serve as semi-visual dividers.

In keeping with the Palo Alto setting and weather, the floor to ceiling wood sliding glass doors can be pushed back and tables are set out under the wood trellis draped with climbing roses. "As one sits and watches the bustling street activity, it is evocative not only of Greek cafes but appropriate for the climate and lifestyle of Palo Alto."

Photography:
Douglas Dun

Etrusca
San Francisco, CA

Design:
Backen Arrigoni Ross
San Francisco, CA

The 142-seat restaurant, just south of Market St. in San Francisco and at the Rincon Center Annex, is a Greek/Italian flavored addition to the Il Fornaio Corp.'s group of gourmet restaurants in California.

The action is in the glass enclosed, exhibition kitchen that appears along one side of the restaurant. A giant rotisserie/oven—under a wonderfully-painted plaster chimney hood—is the central focus with other grills and oven, and marble topped prep tables flanking it.

In the restaurant proper, the walls have marble wainscots and birds-eye maple panelling outlined in ebony. The coffered ceiling replays the same pattern and materials. Marble topped counters, brass railing and the rich, terra cotta colored terrazzo floors are all enhanced by the custom copper light fixtures that add a dramatic glow over the proceedings below.

Picking up on the copper motif of the walls and ceiling are the ebony trimmed booths that run the length of the restaurant under the disk-like lighting fixtures. They cleverly divide the space into "private" enclosures and the booths are accented with birds eye maple strips and ivory colored squares. Black leather-like upholstery is used on the booth seating and to upholster the dark wood colored chairs lined up with white covered tables along the long walls of the space. The "Greek/Italian" tradition is emphasized in the specially commissioned murals and the vases and urns that are displayed in the black and glass vitrines in front of the exhibition kitchen.

Two bars were designed to accommodate the restaurant. The upper level bar offers cocktails and light appetizer service while the low-level bar is used for the dining room customers.

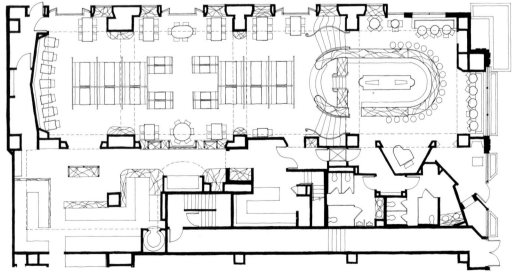

Photography:
Douglas Salin

The Tapas Barcelona Restaurant features regional Spanish tapas (hors d'oeuvres) and mariscos (seafood) with a special emphasis on the unique cuisine of Catalonia of which Barcelona is the capital. What Marve Cooper Design, the design firm, has achieved is to create an authentic Barcelona tapas bar that captures the avant garde modernism of that cosmopolitan city.

Marve Cooper's visit to that city inspired him and helped him to capture the Catalan spirit, and the mixture of influences evident in the art galleries and cafe scenes. He has translated the excitement, color and spirit of the modernist movement that exploded in Barcelona in the late 1970s and it is comparable to what happens in the social and nightlife scene in Paris in the late '20s-early '30s.

The exterior of the restaurant is painted black and brilliantly illuminated by giant, six foot tall letters that spell out the cafe name in a most graphic manner. To emphasize the "vibrancy and movement" inside, there are rich mosaics, ribbons of neon and slotted walls and ceilings. Brick, cement block and richly-painted accent walls are adorned with posters and Bohemian sketches imported from Barcelona and collages by Filip Sotirovic.

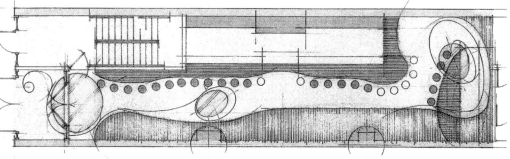

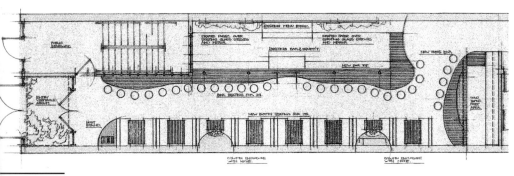

The street level of the two story restaurant is dominated by a 12 ft. tapas bar, encased in glass and surrounded by a sunrise of mosaic mirrors, hanging dried salt cod. Serrano ham and chorizo. The 30 ft. cocktail bar, also on this level, is constructed of wood, copper and tile. For seating there are wooden booths covered with art painted fabrics. The scene is illuminated by custom designed light fixtures.

Up on the second level there is a variety of seating possibilities in the long, narrow space that range from modern carved upholstered booths to intimate seating areas with banquettes for lounge-style dining to the traditional dining tables and chairs. The undulating lines recall Gaudi's sculptural park benches and a rain forest diorama adds visual impact.

Each level is 2000 sq. ft. and 65 patrons can be accommodated on the main level between the booths, the bar and the cocktail bar while the upper level seats 50.

Photography:
Mark Ballogg
Steinkamp/Balogg
Chicago, IL

Lulu
San Francisco, CA

Design:
Cass Calder Smith Architects, Inc.,
San Francisco, CA

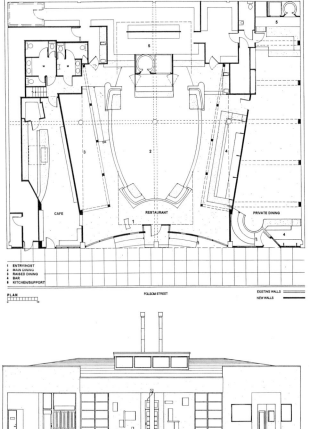

PLAN

1 ENTRY/HOST
2 MAIN DINING
3 RAISED DINING
4 BAR
5 KITCHEN/SUPPORT

FOLSOM STREET

EXISTING WALLS
NEW WALLS

CAFE   RESTAURANT   PRIVATE DINING

The design firm, Cass Calder Smith Architects, took its inspiration for Lulu—located in the Yerba Buena district of San Francisco—from Michelangelo's 1536 design for the Piazza del Camidoglio in Rome. Basically, the design calls for a trapezoid-shaped plan with a centralized ellipse.

"Through layering the existing and the new, the composition emerged. The interplay of figure and ground as well as people and objects is expressed through the dramatic composition of the space and the activities it contains." First, the designers overlaid the trapezoid plan onto the 8000 sq. ft. warehouse structure's plan and this defined the main restaurant and the adjacent retail spaces. The existing double barrel vault ceiling was "peeled" open at the front and rear to admit sunlight—and "reveal the activity within."

The new front wall was bowed inward "to invite passage and movement." The elliptical-shaped main dining room is central in the plan with a free standing raised dining area on the left and a bar on the right. These angle apart and focus onto the exhibition kitchen—and emphasizes it just as Michelangelo's plan brought the Senatoro building into prominence in the Roman plan. From the exhibition kitchen "emerges the food which fuels the celebration of the sacred and the mundane."

The main, centrally-located dining room—two steps down from the adjacent areas, can seat 90 at tables of mahogany and maple and chairs upholstered in black and white leather. The booth seats are upholstered in a blue and black striped fabric. The left side "raised" dining area can accommodate 40 diners in a

"building within a building" which evokes images of the rustic Italian countryside. Here, the tables are distressed fir, the chairs are ash ladder backs, and the walls glow with golden plaster finishes. Forty can also be seated at the bar which is reminiscent of Harry's Bar in Venice. This area is 1960-ish: cool, clean and square with mahogany, glass, yellow stained maple, blue leather and chrome furniture.

The kitchen, the central focus of all three areas, features a fire brick, wood burning oven and a giant rotisserie for whole chickens and loins of pork.

Throughout the restaurant the integral colored plaster walls blend comfortably with the colored concrete floors and the vaulted ceilings of sandblasted Douglas fir.

For decorations, the designers selected "scenes from the Riviera taken from films of Fellini mingled with the industrial images of Raymond Loewy." They create a space where "a daily urban drama unfolds between harmony and chaos in this fire-lit, Mediterranean scene."

Photography:
Michael Bruk

Frantoio
Mill Valley, CA

Design:
Cass Calder Smith Architects
San Francisco, CA

The inspiration for Frantoio Ristorante, a Bay Area restaurant, evolved from a tour of Tuscany and a stay in a 1000 year old villa. "The architectural elements grew from a vision of a Tuscan-spirited place, rich in the imagery of the region's farms and hill towns, yet merged with a contemporary metropolitan ambience."

The spacious "refined-rustic" main dining room is a non-literal interpretation of a Tuscan farmhouse with a 27 ft. high timber trussed roof, terra cotta floors and latticework. The focal point is the "Frantoio"—the glass-enclosed olive oil production room and the pair of four ton, Italian granite olive crushing wheels that were the starting point of the whole project. The Frantoio is a room within a room with a 24 ft. glass facade containing the imported hydraulic-powered crushing and pressing machinery. Chardonnay-colored, custom made, ceramic tiles cover the walls of the Frantoio.

The restaurant that surrounds the oil production center also features wood fired, Roman brick pizza and rotisserie ovens, custom wood and steel tables and raised booth seating. The long, low barrel vaulted bar area is defined by sleek lines and '90s finishes. This room is finished in white maple and burgundy dyed wood work and furnished with abundant banquette seating and contemporary black metal furniture.

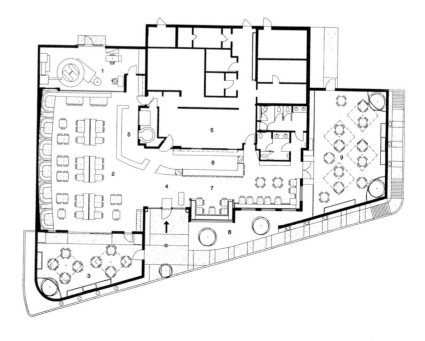

Photography:
Michael Bruk,
San Francisco, CA

Embracing both the dining room and the bar are intimate dining gardens "creating an inside-outside connection that is characteristic of Tuscan farmhouses." The gardens overflow with olive trees, fountains, rosemary and lavender all of which serve as a barrier from the road while providing delightful vistas for the diners inside.

"Historically arch-typical and at the same time modern, the space achieves a dynamic balance that is set into motion with the emergence of food and olive oil, people and production, and the memories and fondness of Italy and California."

Design:
Aria Group Architects
Oak Park, IL

Located in what was 70 years ago built as a warehouse, is the now fashionable, 120-seat restaurant that features Northern Italian cuisine at moderate prices. This "old/new" concept is carried out throughout the design as the designers combined the old with the new in the furnishings, the textures, the lighting and the decorations.

The open design maintains the exposed brickwork and ductwork of the once warehouse. "We wanted Cucina Paradiso to be refreshing in its simplicity. We kept the lines clean and simple yet comfortable and let the food be the star." The sunny golden/olden facade is accented with sleek black awnings and a colorful frieze above. The marble entry leads patrons into "a fusion of past and present." The rough, brick textured look of the original warehouse is contrasted with the soft flow of fabric "waves" that affect the undulating "ceiling." The modern tension cable lights are symbolic in that they refer back to the structural tensioning system of the original structure. Also emphasizing the "roots in the past" is the custom painted mural of "Mother Cucina" in her kitchen as an illustration of the history of Italian cooking traditions.

Raised up from the concrete floor is the bar where the floor is patterned in alternating stripes of cherry and maple stained wood. "This transition plays off the fabric canopy overhead which blankets its own concealed lighting thus creating an intimate ambience." Reflective of the upbeat and contemporary vision of the restaurant's owners, Lee Magnuto and Anthony Gambino, is the modern, stainless steel pasta sculpture which contrasts with the walls. The light-looking black lacquered chairs attend the sharp white linen.

"The melding of different eras is key in creating a young, hip, urban dining place in traditional

Photography:
Charlie Mayer

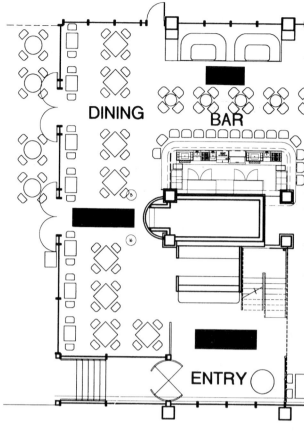

Marve Cooper, the noted Chicago-based restaurant designer, has "fused the mysterious outer galaxies with vibrant Mediterranean colors and the abstract imagery of ancient Rome" to create the unique setting of Azio, in the Peachtree Center in Atlanta.

The space was originally conceived to house a bank which made it difficult to create a sense of warmth and intimacy in the high, open allotted space. The design team solved this problem by adding a barrel vaulted ceiling and then painting it a deep blue color. This "blue Mediterranean sky" was studded with twinkling star-lights and luminous, three-tiered spherical lamps. With the "sky" in the design, the designer could "encompass the essence of escape, fantasy and travel as seen by ancient poets and through the telescope of the 17th century astronomer Galileo."

The design team blended a palette of bold primary colors with neutral tones to suggest a "modernist" style. Gold capped, blue/gray columns — contemporary interpretations of classic elements—anchor the room

and the subtle, creamy faux painted walls are adorned with abstract paintings and murals with symbols and the colors of ancient Rome. The featured open kitchen with its wood burning stove is framed by rows of yellow and red vinegar bottles lined up like sentries.

The handsome wood bar is enhanced with a geometric blue and gold design, and hanging over the bar is an arched copper ceiling faux painted in a yellow-green fusion. Repeating the circular global motif that appears throughout this "galaxy"-inspired design are the golden ringed bar stools around the bar.

Marve Cooper says that surfaces must stimulate the customers, so layering with pictures or drapery is necessary. Using drapes and columns, the designer was able to artistically divide the cavernous space into warm, intimate and romantic areas.

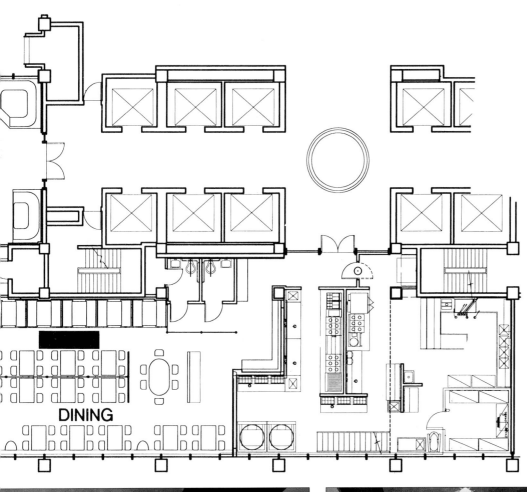

Project Designer:
Grace Kuklinski Rappe

Product Manager:
Stan Percel

Project Architect:
Wright Architects,
Atlanta, GA

RTKL Associates,
Dallas, TX

Creative Forms:
Creative Arts Unlimited,
St. Petersburg, FL

Faux Finishes:
Kozan Studios,
Chicago, IL

Photography:
Mark Ballogg,
Steinkamp/Ballogg,
Chicago, Il

DINING

The area of West Columbia, in South Carolina, is experiencing a new growth and revitalization and this 3600 sq. ft. space, formerly occupied by another restaurant, was assumed by a new owner. The new restaurateur wanted a design that would "create a vibrant atmosphere which reflects the changing attitude of the community—while maintaining the integrity of the building shell." The task, with an extremely limited budget, fell to the Johnson Studio of Atlanta.

William Johnson, the principal of the design firm, and his staff opted to highlight the existing elements such as the exposed brick walls, the wood beam filled ceiling, and the rich outpouring of natural daylight through windows and existing skylights. By manipulating the space and by the brave use of bold colors, the designers then added liberal touches of copper and stainless steel to achieve a contemporary atmosphere juxtaposed with the existing rustic elements. The modern light fixtures fill in where daylight leaves off—or supplements light where needed.

The designers affected a festive and lighthearted space with interesting and unique elements such as the "Tuscan" columns and the hand-painted frieze—all accomplished by local artisans and craftspeople. The effective interior design complements the Tuscan cuisine and also sets Mangia! Mangia! apart from its neighbors.

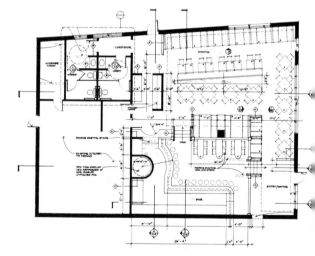

Principal:
William E. Johnson, III

Project Architect:
William Jay George

Design Assistant:
Jennifer L. Hall

Photography:
Robert Clark, Robert Clark Photography, Columbia, SC

Design:
Mesher Shing & Associates
Seattle, WA

Created for Schwartz Bros. Restaurants-also the owner of Spazzo-is Cucina! Cucina!, an Italian cafe concept that made its first appearance in Seattle in 1988.

This job, for the Bellevue location, entailed the development of a new Italian restaurant concept that could be expanded nationally. Each location will have its own distinct personality and be reflective of its local environment, but certain elements will be consistent such as the open kitchen, the exposed wood burning ovens, and the excitement and theater created by the "energetic culinary activities."

To further the "lively atmosphere for family and friends," the restaurants will feature open, naturally-illuminated spaces accented and enlivened with murals, collages, bicycles suspended overhead along with oversized pasta and olive oil decanters. Instead of dark, staid chairs and furniture, the everyday "seat" becomes another colorful element in the already happy, colorful environment.

Light natural knotty pine is used for the divider booth seating on the floor, for the special bar area and at the curved counter that also serves as a low, semi-divider in front of the open kitchen. A light teal/green color appears on the columns which are capped with rings of red and yellow. The same green is used to accentuate the comfortable, woven rattan chairs. The Italian flag colors-red/white/green-tastefully modified, band the tablecloths and reappears in a watery wash over the arched ceiling in the main dining room.

For the young and impatient diners, tables are covered with butcher paper and crayons are provided for the budding artists or the inveterate doodlers. A spin-off of this concept is Cucina! Presto!: a kiosk concept featuring a limited fast-food menu of take-out semi- or fully-prepared sauces, pastas, pizzas and entrees. The kiosk will be located in supermarkets, food courts and strip centers.

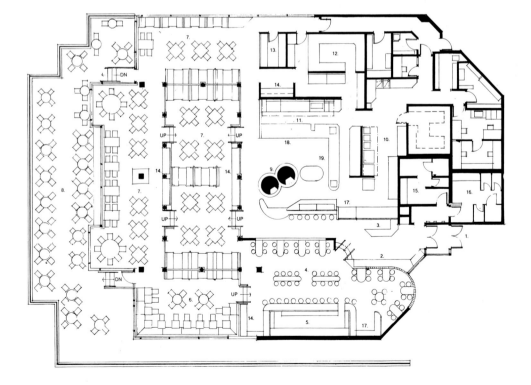

Photography:
Dick Busher, Seattle, WA

Il Fornaio is a popular chain of restaurants/delis/take-outs located throughout Southern California. Each Il Fornaio looks different and has a different texture though they were all designed by Backen Arrigoni Ross, the San Francisco-based design firm. For the newly-opened Burlingame restaurant, the location that was selected was an old, existing structure that had housed, in the past, a series of failed enterprises. The design challenge was to remove the finishes from all the previous remodels and get back to and maintain the original structure's design.

The new Il Fornaio Cucina Italiano is the result of the stripping away of the previous finishes and the exposing of the building's surfaces. "The exposed structure becomes the restaurant aesthetic making the space feel historic and genuine." Once again we find a return to earthy materials, natural textures, a fondness for wood woven baskets, brick and concrete.

Large sliding windows open up the restaurant to the active street life. The old brick facade with the wide spanning arched openings are filled in with low flower boxes that separates the outdoor sidewalk cafe from the indoor lounge area just beyond. The cafe is furnished with woven rattan and metal chairs and glass topped stainless steel cafe tables. "The cafe atmosphere of the loggia and the sidewalk tables is inviting to passersby."

Inside, under the high, metal trussed ceiling that hovers over the retail/deli/bakery part of Il Fornaio, the black square "dots" on the white mosaic tiled floor are accented by the deep borders and wide cuffs of small black tiles.

The counters and glass covered refrigerated display cases and some of the walls are covered with large white square tiles. The smooth, slick surface is complemented by the natural wood moldings, frames, doors, windows and cabinets and the plethora of plaited bushels and baskets, dried herbs and spices, black iron racks

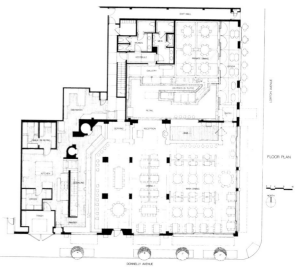

and hooks and the pendant white globe lighting fixtures. Together they suggest a wholesome, old-fashioned smelly-but-sweet Italian neighborhood grocery store.

In the elevated bar and restaurant dining areas, heavy wood timber beams rest on corrugated, terra cotta building block columns and supporting "partitions" while slabs of lumber criss cross over the "ancient" beams. The stained and "weathered" concrete floors are inset with strips of wood and knotty pine dividers serve to separate the light maple and rush chairs and white clothed tables into more "private" groupings.

Here, too, the lighting combines general indirect lighting that dramatizes the architectural features with direct spot lighting which places a pool of light on each table.

Atmospheric old framed photographs fill some of the walls in the dining area but mainly the terra cotta partitions and columns leave lots of openings so that diners have unobstructed views into the retail store, the kitchen and all the bustling activity that makes Il Fornaio so popular.

Photography:
Douglas Dun

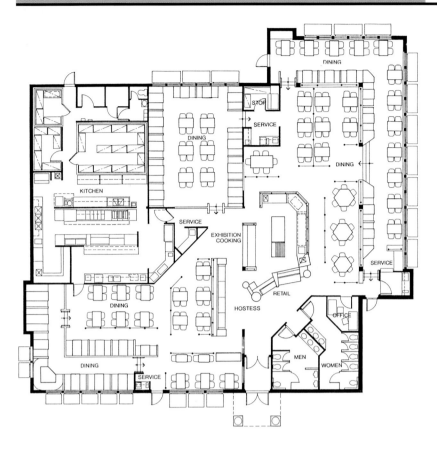

This fun and imagination filled 8400 sq. ft. family-style, Italian restaurant has been described as an Italian version of Willy Wonka's Chocolate Factory—but here the end product is home-cooked Italian dishes. The designers, Cornoyer-Hedrick, turned the familiar into something new, fresh and exciting by adding a "fantasy adventure into the warehouse of food invention."

The uniqueness of the design depends upon the bright, strong colors and the larger-than-life scale of ordinary objects made extraordinary. The giant kitchen utensil take on definite, eye-arresting personalities as they hang down from the high ceiling. In some instances the designers have created "characters" by combining the common elements: forks for hands, flour sifters as heads, and cheese graters as bodies. Even the lamp fixtures become special since they were fabricated out of commercial restaurant colanders.

Bright colors are splashed over the design; on the multi-hued furniture; on some of the "artifacts"; and on the walls—"further stimulating excitement." Some walls feature stained wood in alternat-

ing colors with a diamond motif while others are brightly painted with waving geometric lines. The same bright colors spill over onto the vinyl upholstered booths which are contrasted with the dark gray table tops and the black lacquered chairs. Even the metal shades of the drop lights pick up the color challenge and respond in kind.

Most of the floor is covered in a battleship gray industrial type flooring while a red and blue patterned carpet is used in the seating area. Overhead, industrial exhaust fans were installed as ceiling fans and framed panels of industrial strength woven metal mesh act as dividers between the booths.

Cornoyer-Hedrick helped name the project, develop the unique visual image, the logo and the Bssghetti people that fill the upper space. They also designed all the special fixtures.

Photography:
Visus, Ltd., Phoenix, AZ

Scala's Bistro
San Francisco, CA

Design:
Backen Arrigoni Ross
San Francisco, CA

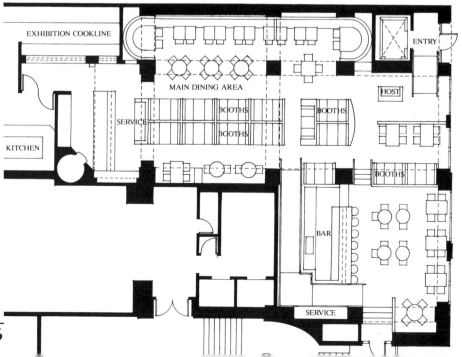

The design firm of Backen Arrigoni Ross was given the assignment of remodeling and recreating the 3400 sq. ft. space in the San Francisco Drake Hotel just off Union Square in San Francisco. The goal was to "create a European cafe or bistro that looked like it had been there for years." All that remains of the original structure—the vaulted plaster ceiling—was restored and highlighted with gilt.

For their palette the design team concentrated on mahogany paneling, a richly colored tile floor, a free use of mirrors, veneer plaster and plaster ornaments and custom light fixtures. All of this is highlighted by the special artwork commissioned from the local artists, Evans & Brown. The large painting of Capri and the spectacular chandelier based on one in Amsterdam's Cafe Americain, are the main focuses in the main dining room. Smoky-hued murals of cafe life and the rich warm glow from the booth and wall sconces in the rear dining room help to create a warm, intimate ambiance. To counterpoint the cozy feeling, there is "the brightly lighted stage of the exhibition cooking area with the activity around the pizza oven; the wrought iron pot rack glittering with copper pans, and the color, aroma and texture of food being prepared."

From the bar which overlooks the dining room, the patron can watch the cable cars making their way up and down Powell St. Here, the "centerpiece" of the space is the tropical still life that dominates one of the walls. The exterior is painted an oxidized red and is modeled after traditional European painted storefronts. The blue awnings, ball lights and applied gilt letters along with the stylized planters all give Scala's Bistro—"a strong visual impact on the street."

Photography:
Douglas Dun

Another blend of cuisines and cultures is Le Colonial: a French/Vietnamese restaurant set on two floors of a renovated town house on fashionable E. 57th St. in Manhattan. The design, by Greg Jordan, gently evokes the architecture and the decorative elements found in French Indonesia at the turn of the last century and the design is based on old picture postcards and faded photos. The "research material" is also used to decorate the interior.

The main dining room is located on the street level and can seat 100 and the main kitchen is located behind it. The concept calls for a "room within a room" with the "native," loft-like architecture seen beyond the "European" addition. This area is paneled with a rough grade plywood to look distressed and old. It is finished in a "tobacco yellow" color with a yellowing polyurethane finish over it. The lower part of the wall is inset with panels of woven straw matting stained mahogany while above, dark green shutters, mounted in "closed" pairs, alternate with panels of mercury mirror.

Reproductions of the aforementioned "research" photos create a decorative scenic frieze around the room. The ceiling of pressed and patterned tin is painted a reddish brown and rotating ceiling fans are suspended from it. The floor is multi-colored tile and wood with dark green woven reed

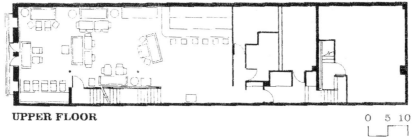

UPPER FLOOR

0 5 10

LOWER FLOOR

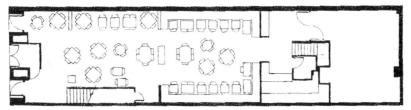

chairs with red and green upholstered pillows and pads set out upon the floor.

A mahogany and off-white staircase with iron balusters imported from France clings to one side of the restaurant and brings diners up to the more casual and relaxed design of the second level. This lounge-like area can accommodate 75 and also has its own, smaller kitchen. Tea, cocktails and light repasts are served in the quiet mustard yellow and brown ambience which is relieved by the daylight that enters through a wall pierced with windows. Rattan lounges and chairs are casually set around the space and rest on oriental-type rugs "scattered" over the dark brown stained wood floors. The ceiling is acoustically treated with tongue and groove, painted wood.

Throughout, potted palm trees add their grace, color and exoticism to the ambience and the lighting in Le Colonial is soft and romantic. The lighting is provided by antique sconces located between the mirrored panels, by pendants with "thatched" shades and brass lamps with green silk, pleated shades lined in warm color.

Photography:
Michael Mundy

Principal:
David Rockwell

Photography:
Paul Warchol

Just as the design blends a high energy Manhattan attitude with the contemporary lifestyle of small city Greenwich, so does the menu combine high style French cuisine with Asian cooking. Baang, in Chinese, means "to bind together" and the tying together here is done with style and whimsy.

The stucco exterior was designed to give the impression that the diner is walking on a typically "old Connecticut street," but once through the authentic old Woolworth's revolving doors—it is all new and very different. A 12 ft. zinc covered hanger door can slide back and connect the restaurant with the patio "creating a New York street cafe effect."

The one, high ceilinged room combines the kitchen, the dining room and the bar areas. It is an intimate "social atmosphere" that encourages patrons to eat, drink, watch others and spend an evening.

The color palette is based on spices: ginger root yellow, chili pepper red, and tones of leek green used on the walls and floor.

The palette is also incorporated in the copper railings that run along the wooden platform that elevates the bar and a major portion of the dining room. "Colored disks are randomly placed—Mondrian style—within the railing in order to evoke a sense of freedom and play." Eighteen foot long copper mesh "clouds" rest atop four oxidized copper poles. They were inspired by Asian pagodas and copper woks.

The theatrical showcase—the open kitchen—is located behind the grand banquette and diners have an unobstructed view of the chefs at work and at wok. Specially-designed plush persimmon colored love seats and the Baang sofa turn the bar area with its curvaceous zinc topped bar into "a warm inviting area in which to relax." Baang is truly a unique blend of design elements and cuisines that make for a memorable dining experience.

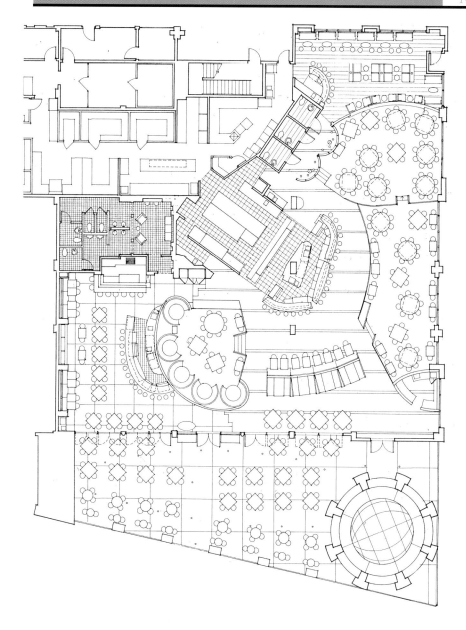

With the China Grill in NYC thriving, the owner of the popular restaurant once again called upon the designer/architect, Jeffrey Beers, to undertake the design of the new China Grill in Miami Beach's hot and sizzling South Beach district. They wanted to create "a new experience—and not a duplication" of what has been so successful in New York. In the 11,000 sq. ft. blueprinted for this restaurant, the architect had to accommodate a main dining room, separate indoor lounge and cafe spaces, an outdoor cafe, two exhibition kitchens, a prep kitchen and seating for 400. The design solution weaves these areas together while subtly separating them by changing floor and ceiling levels. Without creating definite visual barriers, fabric drapes and translucent panels do affect intimate seating arrangements.

The sidewalk cafe, out front, is defined by the colored concrete and the sharp black awnings over the stainless tables and chairs. The interior design is "centered" on the large exhibition kitchen which is framed by the cherry-wood topped bar/counter and massive bowed "shoji" screens that are back lit. In order for diners to enjoy the full theatrical experience, the seating in the

main dining area is raised to three separate levels of limestone flooring with marble inlays that quote passages from Marco Polo's travel journal.

Bronze and stainless steel railing contain each level as do the defining zig-zag silhouetted mahogany covered columns.

"And Zen Sum" cafe is a more casual dining area within the restaurant and it is raised up even further from the limestone paved level. Brass chopsticks are embedded in the terrazzo floor, wood wall panels are finished in birds eye maple, and five curved upholstered booths with mahogany backs create an arced low divider wall around the elevated bar that services the 45-seat area. A sheer fabric drape, suspended around the front of the space, can be "closed" to create a more intimate or private party setting.

Another raised dining area/lounge/bar that can seat 42 patrons is located at the far end of the room opposite the entrance. A screen of cherrywood dividers "separates" the area which features assorted vivid blue patterned upholstery fabrics on the chairs and sofas.

The teak flooring is compatible with the mahogany, the silvery gray accent fabrics, and the panels of woven rattan. The lighting throughout this most contemporary "Chinese Restaurant" highlights accents, separates and unifies the total dining experience.

Design Team:
Jeffrey Beers, Timothy
Schollaert, Seung Jae Lee

Architect of Record:
Todd B. Tragash, S.T.A.
Architectural Group

Photography:
Paul Warchol

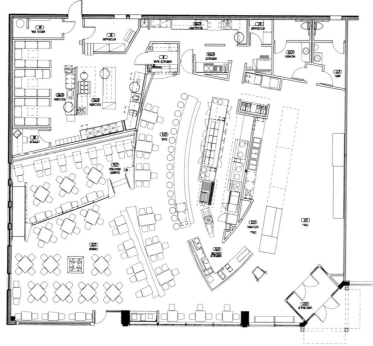

Leeann Chin's name is well known and respected in the Minneapolis-St. Paul area and it is almost synonymous with great Chinese take-out food. She called upon Shea Architects to develop a new prototype restaurant and this Asia Grille, located in Eden Prairie, is the design that will be appearing in many places across the country. The Grille features an open display cooking area where the food is prepared while the diners watch. In addition, the designer included a bar, a take-out counter, and even a small but select market for Asian specialties. The cuisine served here is a blend of five Asian countries.

The neutral color scheme combines warm whites and deep grays with assorted natural wood tones. They range from the blonde wood table tops to the medium brown wood on the partial dividers and backing up the upholstered banquettes on the mezzanine level. The open kitchen is fronted by a wood, granite and glass display counter which is illuminated from above by drop lights.

A gray/black terrazzo patterned floor is laid on the heavily trafficked aisle in front of the kitchen. The lighting throughout is warm and sparkles with low voltage halogen highlights to create a warm and relaxing ambience in which to watch the theatrics of the kitchen.

Mark Miller, the internationally known chef and restaurateur, has come up with another entertaining and patron involving dining concept, and the design team, Adamstein & Demetriou, has provided the exciting architectural design to match. Based on the street foods of Japan, China, Thailand, Korea and Malaysia, Raku's menu features "common dishes" given new meaning by the chef and the designers have taken the mundane "diner" and elevated to a sublime setting where the food preparation is as much of an attraction as the food itself.

Adamstein & Demetriou have drawn inspiration from the rich imagery of the East to create this multi award winning restaurant. The focal element of the space is the massive copper hearth and grill with the wrap-around counter. This is complemented by the glowing rice paper screens around it and the giant open parasols-randomly suspended from the ceiling-create vivid splotches of red, orange and gold. The architects/designers have combined traditional and contemporary imagery of bamboo, moss, paper, stone and wood lattice screens to create an interior that is sensual and exciting. Adding to the show and the kitchen showmanship is the added attraction of video screens alive with scenes from classic Japanese movies and cartoons. The restaurant is filled with the eclectic sounds of jazz, Japanese pop and Asian dance music.

The 3000 sq. ft. restaurant can seat 60 inside and another 40 outside-weather permitting. There is a choice of high stool or low stool seating, with appropriate height counters, as well as bench-like arrangements.

The Noodle Bar is surrounded by a high stool counter while in the bar there are standing tables and high stool counters. An "Express" concept for Raku is in the works which will roll out in 1000 sq. ft. spaces located in commercial areas.

Designers:
*Theodore Adanstein,
Olvia Demetriou*

Photography:
Theodore Adamstein

The 150 seat Korean restaurant, located in Washington, DC, attracts customers that live and work in this prestigious Foggy Bottom neighborhood. The "star attraction" is food prepared at tables equipped with down-draft, hood free, "Roaster Tech" grills that eliminate the grease and smoke one usually anticipates when visiting a Korean restaurant.

The front room of Jin-Ga features a makore wood and black granite bar. Four "Roaster-Tech" equipped tables are located along outside perimeter windows opposite the bar and banquettes and additional 16 Roaster-Tech tables are in the main dining room. Makore clad credenzas serve as bases for the columns sheathed in the same wood.

Here are displayed Korean art and artifacts as well as floral arrangements. Blending with the makore panels and the wood covered walls are the black edged and natural wood toned laminate topped tables. The primary color scheme is muted plum and sage. Assorted subtly patterned fabrics are used to cover the banquettes and chairs but the bar stools are covered with sage faux leather.

The custom colored carpet is patterned in colors complementary to the upholstery and the details. Throughout, ambient light filters down from the newly added coved ceiling and it mixes with the abundant natural light that streams in during the daylight hours. Bamboo details, stone lanterns, three tatami rooms and a tranquil oriental garden complete the 8500 sq. ft. restaurant.

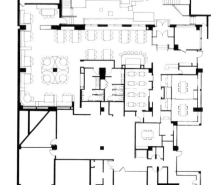

Sr. Designer:
Gustin Tan

Photography:
*Dan Cunningham,
Arlington, VA*

Benihana Restaurant
Piccadilly, London, England

Design:
International Design Group
Toronto, ON Canada

Long familiar for its table-top, hibatchi style cuisine and with outposts located around the world, Benihana recently opened just minutes away from bustling Piccadilly Circus on Sackville St. in London. Though the address was prime, the actual space presented problems: a poor storefront configuration, a fragmented interior and varying floor levels that compromised the quality of the service.

The designers opened up the restaurant with wide areas of fenestration to either side of the central, glass doored entrance. The bright lights and the blaze of rich color from within beckons to people on the street. Visible from the street also is the sinuously curved, perforated stainless steel bar under a floating dropped ceiling. The design firm, International Design Group, opted for a circular plan treatment with a pathway paved in blue tiles that takes the diner through the space and floating "skylights" up above light up the path. An elegant ramp, at the rear of the restaurant, makes a smooth transition between the two floor levels and it repeats the same circular motion. "It looks like the whole space is 'moving' around the core." The restaurant is finished in a rich Pompeian red color with other sumptuous color glazes added for interest.

The "theater" and "excitement" takes place at each hibachi topped table where the mobile chefs perform their razzle-dazzle chopping, dicing and flipping acts to the accompaniment of the sizzle of the hidden flames beneath the griddles. If the "performance" ends at one table there is sure to be a repeat performance coming to a nearby table. The often communal tables add a sense of camaraderie to the dining experience. The total design package has given Benihana a modern and entertaining ambience.

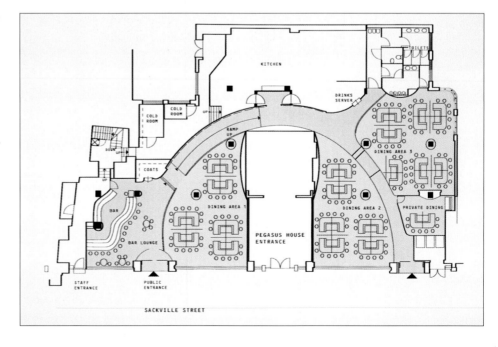

Designer in Charge:
Constantza Carsten

IDG Team:
David E. Newman

Architect:
*Carnell Green
Partnership, England*

Photography:
*Mik Milner Photography,
England*

The Avex Group is one of Japan's leaders in entertainment, music recording and video production. They called upon Interspace Time of Tokyo to create a place "to showcase their talent and say that they are on the cutting edge of entertainment." The result is Velfarre: a teppan-yakki restaurant, a concert hall, a disco, private bar-and more. Kyoka is the teppan-yakki restaurant in the entertainment complex.

Stom Ushidate, the project director, proceeded on an "architectural genesis" from the excavation where tunnels and catacombs were discovered 20 meters below the street level. Artifacts from a multi-national culture were found suggesting that the catacombs

were originally used for entertainment. Inspired by 8th-12th century architecture, Ushidate created a "contemporary classicism of Moorish design." There is an interplay of Earthtone marble and black granite, of black granite to cracked glass-cracked glass to aluminum-to various fabrics, woods, etc.-"encapsulating an environment of pleasure and entertainment."

The entrance to Kyoka is circular with mustard yellow marble and black granite alternating bands on the walls, black granite floors and a dark ceiling accented with a specially designed light fixture. Inside, the restaurant's floors are ocher marble, and the walls are covered with sycamore panels

with a random pattern inlay of mahogany. The eating bar and the teppan-yakki cooking tops are faced with polished aluminum and the exhaust grilles above are finished with a blue tinted, baked enamel fascia and an aluminum bar embossed with "pictographes." Polished aluminum is also used for the mirror frames, flower holders and for furniture accessories throughout.

The chairs have black leather seats, black painted metal legs and maple wood chair backs. The bar is a combination of black granite and mustard colored marble with a white hue glass back bar.

The cooking experience provides the entertainment for the evening with the diners sharing the experience in this unique multi-level multi-purpose entertainment center.

Principal in Charge:
Stom Ushidate

**Executive V.P.
Architecture:**
Robert R. Lowe

Executive V.P. Interiors:
Hiroyuki Kawano

Photography:
Nacasa & Partners, Inc.

Design:
L. Bogdanow & Associates, Architects
New York, NY

The small, 600 sq. ft. Japanese restaurant, Katana, located on Prince St. in the Soho section of Manhattan, is a jewel-box setting for "Kaiseki." Kaiseki is a traditional Japanese cooking method which translates roughly to "many flavors." Many different dishes, designed by the chef, are served in small portions and there can be from six to ten courses at a dinner. The selection changes nightly.

The scale of the restaurant is distinctly Japanese: like a garden this tiny room seats only 30 and it is meant to create a "quiet, restful and reflective environment." Contrasting with the black and white tile "butcher" floor-found in many older NYC commercial buildings-is the handwoven rush matting used on the ceiling.

The latter choice was inspired by a photograph of a grass cloth floor in a traditional Japanese home. Adding to the cool, serene and garden-like ambience is the pale celadon green walls. The old fashioned windows of the existing store front are covered with wooden venetian blinds that not only complement the restaurant's total design concept, but are also compatible with the neighborhood.

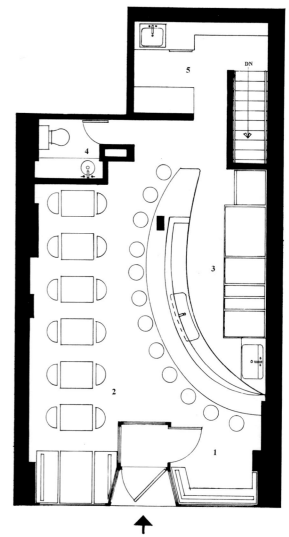

Principal:
L. Bogdanow

Design Team:
Warren Ashworth &
Cathy Van Reenhan

Photography:
Robert Blosser & Cathy
Van Reehan

The 120-seat Eating Factory is a unique concept in Japanese dining in that it combines a "serve-your-self," buffet-style, sushi restaurant with an industrial warehouse architectural setting. The Eating Factory originated in Santa Monica and for the move into this 5500 sq. ft. space, the owner called upon Hatch Colasuonno of Marina Del Rey to introduce some California sun bright colors into the sometimes gray Northwest location.

Color is everything and everywhere under the exposed open ceiling of HVAC systems, ductwork, pipes and structural supports—all painted deep gray. The designer, Luis Colasuonno, used the gray color on the floors, walls and ceiling to "neutralize" the space and to enhance the factory or warehouse feeling. The cement floor is broken up with a grid of red and ocher-gold lines, and the walls are mottled, textured and faux painted with many colors and techniques—all bright, fresh and California in spirit. These splotches of strong color cut down on the need for "artwork."

Justin Henderson, reporting on this project in Hospitality Design said that the designers created "a dynamic non-rectilinear circulation pattern and then created the kinetic architectural geometry needed to keep it in motion." Throughout the space there are a variety of planes and three dimensional forms—some solids and some with cut-outs—that establish the individual areas within

FLOOR PLAN
Scale: 1/16"=1'-0"

the total space and also "human-ize" the scale of the project.

The diner enters into a curved reception area where a green painted bowed partial wall provides "windows" through which to view the restaurant and the raised level of seating. The flow between the buffet and the salad/fruit bar is directed by the low voltage lamps over them and the convex curve that ends the sushi buffet. Inexpensive materials make impressive design statements in the Eating Factory: birch

plywood veneer is used for the counters and the booth seating where the light color of the wood is contrasted with the black upholstery. Diners may opt for the aforementioned booths or for the free standing, dark laminate topped tables on black metal bases that go with birch colored chairs. The pendant light fixtures not only provide the ambient light, they also help to create areas of seating.

As if the color, the forms and the active buffet were not enough to keep the patron entertained, there is an open kitchen—behind the buffet—where the show never stops.

Project Team:
Luis Colasuonno, Harriet Hatch, Hannah Lee, John Egan

Photography:
Marvin Rand